ALWAYS CARRY

YOUR

TORCH HIGH

ALWAYS CARRY

YOUR

TORCH

HIGH

George Lee Foley

authorHOUSE®

AuthorHouse™ LLC
1663 Liberty Drive
Bloomington, IN 47403
www.authorhouse.com
Phone: 1-800-839-8640

Published by AuthorHouse 01/08/2014

ISBN: 978-1-4918-4679-7 (sc)
ISBN: 978-1-4918-4680-3 (e)

Library of Congress Control Number: 2013923468

TABLE OF CONTENTS

DEDICATION

This autobiography is dedicated to my wife of twenty-seven years, JoAnne Ward Foley of Andalusia, Alabama. She has been a blessing, helper and friend.

A special thanks to Dr, Calvin Reid, M.D. for saving my life in April 2012. I thank God for all my doctors. Thanks to Dr. J. Benjamin Craven, M.D., my cardiologist, Dr. Nancy Weaver, M.D., ER cardiologist, Dr. Jasper, M.D., ER physician, Thanks to Dr. Warren Thompson, M.D., my retina physician, Dr. Jorge Arango, M.D. of Retina Associates, and the entire staff. Thanks to Dr. J. Wallace, M.D., my Eye Specialist, Dr. McDonald, M.D., ER physician. Thanks to Dr. Weiser, M.D. of Flowers Hospital for his excellent care when I was treated for a head injury. Thanks to

Internal Medicine Associates of Dothan, Alabama and the entire staff for their follow-up care.

Flowers Hospital, Dothan, Alabama Food and Nutrition Supervisor Darlene Long, Diet Specialist Jasmine, Cashiers: Alicia, Tyler, Tammy, Kelley, Heather and Takela for their excellent service. Thanks to the cooks and the entire kitchen crew. I would like to thank our church, Ridgecrest Baptist Church, Dothan, Alabama for their prayers, visits, and care in our goal toward spiritual maturity. A special thanks to Senior Pastor Ray Jones, Executive Pastor Chuck Locke, Minister to Music and Worship Tim Willis, Minister to Pastoral Care Orin Barrett, Minister of Recreation Bob Sanders, Minister of Education and Discipleship Aaron Dickinson, Minister of Administration Charles Olive, Minister to Students Lloyd Blank, Adult Mobility Trainer Libby Sanchez, the Adult Mobility Class and the entire Church Staff.

I also dedicate this to a fellow co-worker, Larry Foor of Albuquerque, New Mexico. He was a pharmacist and I was the delivery-man at a local pharmacy. I am thankful for his friendship, hunting trip, and for the encouragement to be the best that I could be.

INTRODUCTION

"Are the struggles, obstacles and afflictions experienced by George Lee Foley, ordinary or extraordinary? He is an excellent role-model for others. No matter the obstacle, whenever others are placed ahead of self, a great blessing and reward is attained. Throughout this book, it is evidenced in the lives of others that were assisted by the principles applied in this book. The theme is from The Holy Bible Hebrews Chapter 12 verses 1-7. (NKJV)"

CHAPTER 1

FAMILY LIFE OF GEORGE LEE FOLEY

George Lee Foley was born to George Albert Foley and Mary Margaret (Eickenbrock) Foley, and weighed six pounds and six ounces at birth. I was the second child to be born to Mary Margaret Foley. His mother met Dr. Patrick Kelly, M.D. and a daughter, Patricia Ann Kelly was born to them in Colorado Springs, Colorado on June 1, 1935. Dr. Kelly was a noted physician in Colorado Springs and wrote several medical journals, and authored a book, "Is there a Doctor in the House?" He was a practicing physician in Colorado Springs, Colorado, and made several advancements in the medical field. Dr. Kelly lived in Colorado until his retirement, and moved to Dublin, Ireland, and lived to be eighty-eight years of age.

In 1940, my mother moved to Denver, Colorado to seek a job as a cook. While in Denver, set met my father, George Albert Foley, and on June 1, 1940, they were married. My father was a self-employed entertainer in the Denver area. After they were married, the family rented a small two bedroom house on North Broadway in Denver, Colorado. Denver is known as the "Mile High City"; and my father, who had an Asthmatic health condition since a young boy, and had been issued a rating of 4-F for the Selective Service for World War I. My father was a twin; however, I could not locate the records since records for that time period were destroyed in the Central Records Holding Office in the "Great San Francisco" fire in 1906. My father stated, he was born July 5, 1893 in Sacramento,

California. My father's siblings were all brothers; Frank, Raymond, Benjamin (Ben), and Albert. My father's brother, Ben had a son, whose name was Clyde (Red) Foley, and was born in the old family city of Berea, Kentucky in 1910. Clyde received the nickname "Red" because; he had more red hair, than any of his brothers. In my study of the family history; "Genealogy", I found that, Clyde (Red) Foley was a noted self-employed entertainer, and was famous for his songs, "Peace in the Valley", and "Chattanooga Shoe-shine Boy". Clyde (Red) Foley retired from the entertainment field and moved due to his poor health to the Indianapolis, Indiana area. He was a fine Christian gentleman, and went to be with his

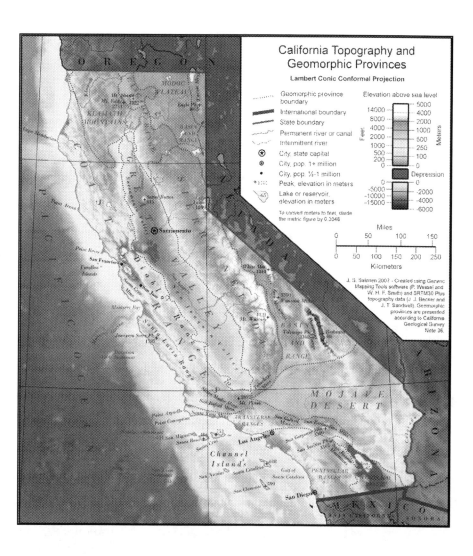

California Topography and Geomorphic Provinces

Lord and Savior in 1968, at the age of fifty-eight. He was an avid baseball fan, and authored several "short stories" about his favorite sport, baseball.

My father, George Albert Foley had a cousin, whose name was George Michael Foley, born in the month of September 1897. He had a daughter named Myrtle Foley, who was born in 1925 and departed this life in 1988 near her family residence in southern California. The records reflect it was San Bernardino, California. I was four years old when my father passed away on August 10, 1945 at Foley's Shoe Service, 512 East Central Avenue, (Highway 66) in Albuquerque, New Mexico.

My mother, Mary Margaret Eickenbrock was born to Bernard and Irene Eickenbrock on January 6, 1906 in Wells, North Dakota. It is with much regret that her mother died while giving birth to her. Her father kept a "Family Diary", and mentioned; my mother, Mary Margaret, weighed only three and one-half pounds at birth. He placed a wooden box, on the kitchen "Pot-belly stove that served as an incubator. She recovered from this very quickly. Her father Bernard was unable to care for her; so she lived with Bernard's brother and his wife, Joseph and Savannah (Tinglehoff) Eickenbrock. Their children were Catherine, John, Benjamin (Ben), Henry and Everett Eickenbrock. The family accepted my mother, as their own, and she had a very happy childhood. When grown, Henry, John and Ben moved to Minneapolis-St. Paul, Minnesota, Catherine moved to St. Cloud, Minnesota, Everett moved to the Seattle, Washington area, and my mother moved to Colorado Springs, Colorado.

My mother moved to Denver, Colorado to seek employment as a cook. She met George Albert Foley, and they were married on June 1, 1940 in Denver, Colorado. Shortly after my parents were married, his doctor advised them to move to a dryer climate. My father accepted Patricia Ann Kelly; my half-sister, as his very own. She went by the last name of Foley. My mother and father rented a small two bedroom house on North Broadway Street, Denver, Colorado. This was about four miles east of the center of downtown.

When I did a Genealogy study of my father's side of the family, I discovered his father's name was N.T. Foley, who was born in London, England in 1830. It is documented that he served as a "Missionary" in Capetown, South Africa. My father mentioned to the family that he was a twin, but I could not locate any documents because, they were destroyed in the "Great San Francisco Fire" in 1906. I researched and could not determine which brother was my father's twin. My father told the family that he had to use church records, and other records, which were "notarized', and served as official verification of birth. My father said he was born July 5, 1893. He had a cousin named George Michael Foley who was born in the month of September 1897.

My father told the family that he had two sons, who served together in the U.S. Navy during the period before World War II. I did not know their names, and I did not have any proof of date of birth for our father.

CHAPTER 2

EARLY LIFE OF GEORGE LEE FOLEY

My life began on a quiet Sunday morning at about 8:30 a.m. on June 22, 1941 at the family residence 739 North Seventh Street, Albuquerque, New Mexico. The doctor advised my mother and father moved from the Denver, Colorado area due to my father's asthmatic condition because the altitude was extremely high. Denver is known as the "Mile High City." They set out in the family automobile, and were headed for; either Arizona or the state of California, since both states have a "dryer" climate. The state of Arizona in the Spanish language means "Arid" or dry. While travelling their automobile broke down, and while waiting for their automobile to be repaired, they observed a few important things. The climate was much better in Albuquerque, New Mexico, and Mr. Foley could breathe much better. At the automobile repair shop, they made friends with a couple, who had two daughters, and they told my family that Albuquerque, New Mexico was a very good place to raise a family, and the cost of living was very low, compared to other places. They had plenty of time, while they were waiting for their automobile to be repaired. My father checked the local newspaper, the Albuquerque Journal, and since he had always had a special interest in being self-employed, he saw a high demand for a shoe-repair business. Across the street from where their friends were staying, my father saw an empty shop. It would make a great location for a shoe-repair shop and it was on Highway 66, about one-half mile east of the center of town. The shop was rented and two shoe-repair machines were bought a very excellent price. Two shoe-repairmen were hired. One was Gene Chavez, who was one of the best, and a relative of Mr. Chavez was hired.

While visiting friends and finding out more about Albuquerque, New Mexico, my father decided to prepare to attend an upcoming auction, that had military homes that were very reasonable, and they had to be moved. The day came for the auction, and my father went with his new friend and arranged to move the newly bought home, after he won the "lowest bid". I remember the day the red truck was moving the newly acquired home to the double-lot my father purchased for our new residence. This was much better than renting, especially for a family man. The house was not a "home" yet, because it was awaiting a new family (ours) to move into. It was about twenty feet across the front and thirty feet from the front to the rear. It was a two bedroom house, bath, large living room, kitchen, and a partially enclosed side porch. The new address was 1604 South Arno Street, and it was a large lot that had a one bedroom house with a detached one car adobe garage, to the rear of the lot. My parents saw it was a good place to raise a family. The double-lot was in a very quiet section, about one and one-half miles south of town. George Lee can still remember the truck that brought the home to the new home site. This was an excellent place to raise children, and the neighbors for blocks around were known by name and were always ready to help each other. My father had always loved to raise animals. He set the area behind the adobe-built single-car garage to raise pigs. I remember he always had a litter of from seven to eight, and they loved to roll in the mud, and they had a large trough (eating-dish). There was room in the pen to keep about fifteen pigs. The truck would come to take them to the plant to have them butchered. This was a very good source of income, as well as food for the table. On the north side, and to the rear, there was a chicken yard, with a building for the chicken to roost, and for the hens to lay their eggs. We had about thirty or more chickens at one time. There was a ramp for the chickens to use to enter their enclosed chicken "coop". When I became older, I helped feed and water the chickens, but I could never prepare one, or kill them. I began raising rabbits, and they would be very easy to care for. I fed them "Purina Rabbit Mix", and always kept their feeding trays and bowls clean and sanitized. One day I decided to raise "bunny rabbits". It—eight to thirty days to be born. For science class, I charted out a "Genetics Chart". The father rabbit was a black, and the mother rabbit was a New Zealand White with "pink" eyes. When I estimated the birth of twelve rabbits, the diagram showed there should be eight white rabbits, and four black rabbits. When they were born, you couldn't tell because they did not have fur until they were about three weeks old. When they were that age, there were: twelve gray rabbits. In genetics, this is called "blending" or an "aleaele". It is a very rare event. I wrote a very good term-paper for Science Class Project and received a very good grade. One day I needed to buy a larger cage, but had no means of getting it home, so I used two of my roller skates, and borrowed two of my sister's roller skates, and placed them under the legs of the cage, and rolled it down the edge of the street for about one-half mile. I enjoyed my time spent raising animals; after becoming a teenager, I decided to devote my time to part-time jobs. It is important at some one time while growing up to learn how to care for animals that you raise or pets. It gives you a feeling of wellness because you are providing for the health and happiness of the animals that you care for.

My friends had a neighbor to Margaret, the daughter of Former President Harry S. Truman. She was getting a new bicycle, and wanted to know if I would like her old bicycle. I said, "Yes, that would very nice." It was a 26" bicycle with a large motorcycle-size seat, but I was so short, I had to get on and off at the ramp at the side of our driveway. I enjoyed that bicycle for a long time, and when the time came to repaint it, I painted it lavender with red trim.

I had the privilege of attending a Dixie-Land Concert which was held at Landmark Park on North Highway 431 in Dothan, Alabama about six years ago where I met several of the entertainers and attendees who knew the Foley Family in Berea, Kentucky. The Foley Estate still stands, and is a very good credit to the entire family. I was doing a Genealogy study of my father's side of the family, and discovered that on my father's side there was Native American Indian. It is believed to be the "Blackfoot Nation". I was looking a each of the five tribes, within the nation, and found a tribe called, "Mountain Man" A picture of an Indian Chief, dressed in "full war bonnet", was almost a positive image of my father. My father's mother's side is thought be "Blackfoot" Indian.

My mother and father moved from Denver, Colorado because of my father's asthma. They were headed to either; Arizona or California, and when their automobile broke down in Albuquerque, New Mexico, the weather was fine for my father's health. I grew up in Albuquerque and I have had asthma since a child, but was never had any ill effects from it.

An addition to the family came on January 8, 1943, when my younger sister, Mary Louise was born. She was born with the same color of eyes as our father, "Green" I was born with "Greenish-Brown" eyes.

My father, George Albert Foley had a cousin, whose name was George Michael Foley, born in September, 1897 and lived most of his life in Kentucky. George Michael Foley had a daughter, Myrtle Foley who was born in Kentucky in 1925, and lived until 1988. She passed away in the San Bernardino; California, and was a fine Christian lady. I remember, she was at the family home in Albuquerque, New Mexico after the funeral of my father in August, 1945.

When my father opened a shoe-repair shop at 512 East Central Avenue in Albuquerque, New Mexico, I did not have the usual baby-sitter, while my parents worked. My father asked the owner of a warehouse a few steps in the rear of their shop, if I could play in the warehouse on a large piece of plywood. My two baby-sitters were two Doberman-Pinchers dogs and they took very good care of me. My father became sick one afternoon about 4:30 p.m. and said to my mother, "Mary, call a taxi, and take the children home, I am having some problems with my asthma." The following morning my mother and two sisters and I arrived at the rear entrance to my father's shoe-repair shop about 8:00 a.m. and my father was lying, face-down and had been bleeding from his mouth. I do not understand why someone did not see he got the proper medical treatment. He is buried across the street from the Albuquerque City Bus Garage on South Yale Boulevard in Albuquerque, New Mexico. When I finished Basic Training in September 1961, I bought and paid for, a beautiful brown marble marker for his gravesite. I could not understand why a marker was not put on his gravesite at the time of the funeral. I will always cherish the memories of my father and his 1933 Hudson Touring Car. It was a four-door and was Hunter Green with Black Fenders. One bit of advice on time with your family, or when you do something for someone or say something about them, "Do it in their "Living Years."

I am very thankful for hard-working parents, and remember both my mother and father arranging to purchase a house from a nearby military auction. My father won the lowest bid and the house was to be moved. It was a two-bedroom, large living-room and kitchen, one bath, and an enclosed back-porch, that was screened half-way. My father bought a large double-lot, and it was zoned for multiple-homes, business and was also zoned agricultural. My father remodeled the existing one-bedroom home to the very rear of our property. My father built an open-front porch, which extended the width of the home. There was also an existing adobe (made from mud) single-car garage. My father saw the opportunity to buy two mobile homes, which were placed between our house and the one-bedroom home in the rear. They made excellent rentals. The small one was a one-bedroom, and the larger one was a two-bedroom. Neither one had an inside bathroom, so my father had Mr. Taylor build a large outdoor bathhouse with one-occupancy restroom and shower facilities. They had privacy since it was a one-occupancy building, it could be locked, when occupied. There was plenty of room for animals. My father bought about six grown pigs, and began raising them to sell and for meat on the table. We also raised several chickens for food and eggs. This was country-living within the city limits. The home was at 1604 South Arno Street in Albuquerque, New Mexico. It was only one and a half miles south of town, and was only one block from the city bus line. We lived two blocks from a public school; and about eight blocks from church and private school.

It was a quiet Saturday morning, and I had a visitor. A black Cadillac stopped in front of our house. I stepped to the sidewalk to greet, my visitor, and the driver opened the back door for his passenger. I said, "Mr. Armstrong, I'm so glad you came to see me this Saturday morning". "Sonny boy, I've come to see Lester Smith". "I will show you where he lives, he lives, next door." "I come from a musical family, will you teach me to sing like you?" "Yes, pick out a song." Like all kids, I was playing, and there goes the black Cadillac. I now had to make it on my own. A few years went by, and I began practicing, a song by Mr. Louie Armstrong, "Hello Dolly". In April 2012, I was invited to sing at "Center Stage", south of Dothan, Alabama, in a Karaoke contest. My first song was "Blueberry Hill" by Fats Domino. When I was finished, I was handed an envelope, I opened it and in it was a prize. I was told to pick out another song, so I put on my "Biker's Bandana", and sang a song by Hank Williams, Jr., "Family Tradition". Next week, I received a Thank you letter and an invitation to sing again. This time I did, Johnny Cash's song, "A Boy Name Sue", and then the next week, I sang, "Hello Dolly" made famous by the Late Great Louie Armstrong. I did it to the memory of my friend, Mr. Louie Armstrong, and to my wife, JoAnne, who was in the audience. I had a great time singing and am blessed with the talent of entertaining inherited from my father, George Albert Foley.

CHAPTER 3

EDUCATIONAL PURSUITS—PREPARATION FOR A LIFELONG CAREER

A person would decide what career they wanted when it came closer to reaching adulthood. Mary Lou, Pat and I went to a private school for grades one through eight, except Mary Lou and I went to the fourth grade to the public school, which was John Marshall Elementary School. Pat was six years older than I, and eight years older than Mary Lou. Pat went to Lincoln Junior High School and then Albuquerque High School until the eleventh and left school to get married at age sixteen. Mary Lou went to Lincoln Junior High for the ninth and to Albuquerque High School for the tenth and eleventh and quit to go to work. She moved back and graduated ten years later in 1971. I went to St. Mary High School on North Seventh Street, in Albuquerque, New Mexico and graduated in May 1959.

My educational goals continued into my adult life because education is a continual plan, and goals change as we grow older. It is important for me to look for the best opportunities, as I become aware that it is a part of my future growth and development. I began attending college right after high school, but soon found out that I did not do well at all. I would have done better going to a trade school. The only reason that I went was because my aunt, Catherine gave me $250.00 to attend college. I began taking college classes in the U.S. Army. My first class was at Mary Hardin-Baylor, with class on Fort Hood, Texas. When in Okinawa, I went to the University of Maryland and studied English. I went to the University of Alaska in Anchorage, Alaska, and took three classes at the Graduate level. My classes have earned me a Bachelor of General Studies (BGS) with a major in Business Administration and a minor in Economics. I graduated in December 1974, and then went to Chapman College (now Chapman University) from March1976 to September 1978. I went to Chapman College at Elmendorf Air Force Base at Anchorage, Alaska, for a total of thirty-six Semester Hours with a Grade Point Average (GPA) of 3.0 on a 4.0 scale. I took the four part written Comprehensive Tests, and earned three A's and didn't pass the Statistics part, because my guidance counselor failed to tell me I was required to take Advanced Statistics. After two heart attacks, and two light strokes, I returned to college to attempt a Master of Business (MBA) for the second time. I earned 13.5 Credit Hours with a Grade Point Average of 3.25 on a 4.0 scale. I enrolled on January 10, 2010 in two Graduate level courses at Westwood College (on-line). I was a candidate for the Master of Business Administration (MBA), and I have earned a 3.0 on a 4.0 scale, and my goal to be an On-Line College is still a dream, I would like to attain, that of Educator. My grades declined because of my health. I earned a C+ at the University of Phoenix. I had another stroke on the day before I turned seventy years of age. I refused to give up, so I enrolled at American Intercontinental University for a class in Decision-Making. I had to drop after the first lesson because the first part of lesson 1, my grade was F, and the second part, I earned an A. I was dismissed due to Physical Disability from Department of Education (Student Aid). I am very blessed because God is a God who wants the best for us. You too can receive God blessings. In the U.S. Air Force, I was required to take the "Professional Development" course. I was required to take the Non-Commission Officer Academy (NCO), but due to my physical restrictions, I was not able to parade march, run, climb, or other strenuous exercise that was required, I was allowed to take this course by correspondence. Education is a continual process; I completed ninety Semester Hours of credit, of which forty-five were for successfully challenging college tests. I challenged Criminology, Geography, History, Physical Education, and several others. If I received a score of seventy percentile or higher, I would be granted, three Semester Hours of credit. I attended the University of Maryland, New Mexico State University, the University of Albuquerque, while serving in the Air Force there. My favorite classes were in Accounting and History. This was before being sent to the University of Nebraska at Omaha for a period of seven months, and I was a student in Business Administration. I graduated with a 2.88 Grade Point Average (GPA) on a 4.0 scale. My degree was a Bachelor of General Studies (BGS) because my classes in business varied, rather than a concentration in one area. However; I did have most of my specialized business classes in Financial Management. I graduated on December 20, 1974. I thought I was finished with my college studies, and the Captain at the Accounting and Finance Office asked me to take an Accounting class with him. It was with Texas State University, when I was transferred to Elmendorf Air Force Base in Anchorage, Alaska, I attended the University of Alaska for three classes, and then nine classes with Chapman College, (Now Chapman University) on base, for a total of thirty-six Semester Hours toward a Masters of Business Administration with a 3.0 Grade Point Average on a 4.0 scale. I grew weary of playing computer games, so at age sixty-nine and one-half, I decided to be an on-line college educator. I began in January 2010 for one year and earned eighteen and one-half Credit Hours to the MBA with a Grade Point Average of 3.05 on a 4.0 scale. I attended Westwood College (on-line), Denver, Colorado and University of Phoenix for a class in Management. I tried going after I had a stroke in June 2011; but my grade of F on the first part of Lesson I, and an A on the second part prevented me from continuing at American International University (AIU) (on-line).

CHAPTER 4

ENLISTMENT IN THE U.S. ARMY

My enlistment in the U.S. Army was on June 30, 1961. My sister Patricia Ann (Pat) came to visit the family about the middle of June, and visited until the first week of July. My Basic Training was from July to September 1961 at Fort Hood, Texas, the largest U.S. Army installation in the world. The Main Gate was at the north part of Killeen, Texas, and was home to the 1st Armored Division and 2nd Armored Division. I was assigned to the 2nd Armored Division, and our Motto was "Hell on Wheels", which was very famous during World War II, and received many awards for bravery, successful battle campaigns, for heroism, both nationally and internationally. Military officers, as well as enlisted personnel were the highest professionally trained soldiers in the world. The U.S. Military Academy at West Point and the Air War College has the best trained combat instructors that could be provided.

My unit that I was assigned to was going to Virginia for Advance Tank Training and Scout Observer Training. I was asked to "waive" my Accounting School at Fort Benjamin Harrison, Indiana because of the shortage of personnel in our unit. I did this, and was enrolled in M-48 Tank Training for eight weeks. The course included ammunition-loading, .50 caliber machine-gun firing, M-60 Tank Gun Firing and Tank Driver. I performed well and all my grades were "excellent" The time came for Graduation Ceremonies. The final task prior to turning in our tank was to clean each of the two tank engine wells. I did a good job on the first. The tank was powered by two 440 cubic-inch Chrysler engines. I was cleaning the second engine well, when the lid to the compartment closed and caught my leg, so I was suspended and could not get out. I yelled for help, and finally two soldiers, who were preparing to go to Tank Graduation, heard me and came to get me loose. The two said, He can't walk up front, and we don't have time to dispatch a vehicle, so we will roll him up front in this wheelbarrow. They rolled me to Graduation, and I graduated.

About two workdays later, the Colonel wanted to see me in his office. I just knew I was in some kind of trouble, but he told me I should be assigned to an administrative job because of the difficulty of cleaning my tank. I was assigned to Supply for about three weeks, and then received a slip telling me to report to Finance and Accounting Office. They had an opening as a Check-writer. I was asked to write the payroll check for $1,000,000.00 (1 million dollars). I did and did not make a single mistake, so I was assigned the job. You see when you give up something like I did, my promised Accounting School, it will come back to you, as something of equal or greater benefit. There was a shortage in the Personnel Office, so I was assigned as temporary duty. I am glad I was selected because one day our Personnel Officer, Mr. Perry asked me to select twelve to be assigned to Germany for a six-month assignment to turn over an American tank unit to the German army, south of Heidelberg, Germany.

I returned to Fort Hood, Texas after my six months in Germany. And was assigned to the Finance and Accounting Office, this assignment was in the Disbursing Section, where I computed payments, Leave and Earning Statement and Regular payroll. My equipment was about as modern as it could come for that period of time. My payroll desk was a desk the size of a TV tray, with a roll of pay vouchers in a box in front of the desk. A manual typewriter was used to fill in the voucher. To the right off my desk, I had a list of the entitlements, deductions, and leave balances for each personnel on the payroll.

I was assign to this base at a very good time, Elvis Presley was there from 1957 to 1959, and I enjoyed the recreation center that he built and paid for called, "Fiddler's Green". It was a million dollar complex, and had four or five large lounges, a private TV room, three or four recording booths, and two listening booths, it had pool tables, backgammon, donuts, pastries, coffee and soft drinks were served. Newspapers, magazines, journals were provided. Each Sunday, after church services you could find me there. When I served two years, I was eligible to sign up again for a choice of job, base, if available. I stopped one day to find out, and reenlisted for another three years. I asked for an assignment to New Mexico, and there was a vacancy at the U.S. Armed Forces Recruiting Station in Albuquerque, New Mexico. My commander was Major Robert B. De Mello, and I was assigned as a Test Proctor. I made several friends while there, Dr. Coova from Chicago, Illinois, Bob Moore, 1st Lt. Miller, George Hurl, Robert Deal, Johnny Johnson and a Navy seaman, we called "Smokey" Burgess. I was very fortunate because, my mother was still living there, so I returned to living at home.

I met and married a young lady, who worked where I did before I joined the Army. She was Frances Christian, a widow with two children, Sandra Bethel, age three and Leo Edward Christian, one year and one-half. We began dating and were married on December 5, 1964. We would have dated longer, but I received orders to go to Okinawa, an island in the South Pacific. I was promoted to Specialist Four (E-4) on 1 January 1965. We rented a three bedroom house at 364 North 64th Street in Albuquerque, New Mexico. I enjoyed living there because it was a quiet neighborhood, and across the highway, there was a target practice area. On Saturdays, I would check-out a .22 rifle and "target practice" for about an hour or two.

In March 1965, we moved to a two-bedroom apartment, since I was going overseas, and the family could not come until I had housing in Okinawa. I ended up moving the family to Peoria, Illinois to be near Frances' sister. I departed for Okinawa in July 1965, and processed in at Oakland Army Terminal in Oakland, California. The navy was looking for volunteers to travel by ship to help decommission, the USNS Patrick. The trip would take approximately thirty days, so I asked to send me by ship. Our first stop was the island of Guam. When we arrived, I put in for a pass and was approved. About three or four of us began walking, and a government mail truck-driver let us ride into town in the back of the truck. He let us out at an A & W Root Beer Stand. I walked to the counter to order, and saw a 1955 Ford with New Mexico license plates. Since New Mexico was my home-state, I wanted to talk to them. We located a couple who owned the car, and they said they were civilian workers there with the government. They invited three of us to tour the island of Guam. The city we were in was the capital city, Aganya. The island was just one of the LD Marshall islands. We began our tour, by heading south to Columbus Park. We drove through the business district and several cars had decal saying U.S. Government Official. Columbus Park was on the western shore of the Pacific Ocean. Across the street were several homes, which were really unique. Each side was painted a different bright color, yellow, pink, blue, and green. The homes were built on poles, and the bottom floor was used for their chickens, rabbits, and other small animals. The people were very friendly, some could speak English, but they spoke a mixture of Spanish and Italian. We then rode to the eastern shore, and stopped for a soft-drink and light lunch. We were invited to swim on the eastern bank of the Pacific Ocean. The water was great, it was about 80 degrees. We rolled up our pants, and kept on our shoes because of the sharp coral on the bottom, otherwise the coral would have cut our feet. After swimming, they took us across the street, and we were asked if we would like a "fresh" coconut. We each got one to take with us.

We arrived back to the shipyard, but before boarding. We spoke with the submarine crew and they asked if we would like to take a look inside the two-man submarine they were cleaning. It was an interesting experience. We boarded the ship, and soon we were fed a good meal in the "Galley" (Dining Hall). We were soon on our way, with our next stop Midway. When we arrived at Midway, we were given a two-hour pass, but it was an escorted military vehicle that took us to a drive-in restaurant for a light meal and when we were leaving, I held out my hand to wave goodbye to some of the island people. I was told by the Navy escort, that that meant that I was ready to fight. I learned fast to be very careful. We boarded the ship again, and we were on our way. Midway is one of the Marshall Islands in the Pacific Ocean.

Our next stop was the Hawaiian Islands, when I inquired we will be arriving at Pearl Harbor. We arrived at Pearl Harbor, just before noon, and we told when you look over the side of the ship you could see the sunken USS Arizona, lost in World War II. Pearl Harbor is on the main island, Oahu. I was eligible, so I put in for a five hour pass. I had a great time. I rented a bicycle near a local park, and rode around for about two hours, watched a baseball game, walked to Waikiki Beach and had a light lunch, visited Fort DeRussey, which is the military high-rise hotel and resort. I was offered by the resort, Fort DeRussey, a tour of Hickham Air Force Base. I was able to do some light shopping, and then we were returned to Fort DeRussey. Since we were in town, I visited the local library and nearby museum and found many interesting things to see. One of the guys from the ship, asked me, "Do you pronounce, this state, "Haviee, or is it "Hawaii?" I said, "Let ask someone that lives here. I asked, and they said, "Haviee", I said, "Thank you", and they answered, "Your Velcomme" Life is great, isn't it?

CHAPTER 5

RETURN TO CIVILIAN LIFE
FROM THE U.S. ARMY

My enlistment completion date in the U.S. Army arrived, and I decided not to reenlist. I was process for separation at Oakland Army Terminal. Our trip from Okinawa was a good trip, and we arrived in San Francisco, California. This was a government contract flight because an airline strike was going on. On July 9, 1966, I was separated and we went to San Francisco to arrange for the trip home. Frances wanted to visit her sister in Peoria, Illinois, and other relatives before moving back to New Mexico. We decided to take the train, since the airline was still undergoing strike. The rates by train were very reasonable. I really enjoyed the train trip. We ate well, and slept right in our seat because the cabins were all booked. We arrived in Peoria, Illinois, in the early afternoon. When I went to claim our luggage, they told me it didn't get taken off, and will be in Joliet, about forty miles north of Peoria, Illinois. The train station manager would arrange for it to be sent back to Peoria, Illinois, but it could take two to three days. After a day visiting her sister, Frances decided she and the children were going to West Virginia to visit the children's grandparents. I didn't care to go, and I needed to stay and get our luggage. The next morning, I decided I wanted to go to the employment office, so I had my brother-in-law take me there. I said, "Yes, I'll go for a job interview". It was for Service Manager, at M & H Equipment Company, a Hyster Lift-truck organization. I got the job, and went to work at 1:00 p.m. the same day. The family was sure surprised. While they were gone, I went downtown and bought me a car. When the family returned, Frances didn't like the car because she couldn't pick it out. I bought it for me, not the family. When she got back I had to exchange it. She and the children picked out a brown 1960 Ford station-wagon. It was a good car, except you could not turn it around in the normal required time. I was not going back to the car-lot for the third time. We went to the supermarket just a few blocks away, and when I stepped up to the butcher counter, there was my friend, and co-worker, Frank. Frank and I worked together in Okinawa, just a couple months before. I am glad to have friends besides the family. We had a great opportunity to buy a two-story, four bedroom; two-bath home, with a large family room, fireplace, and front porch that extended the completed front of the house. We paid $12,900.00 and it was a very good buy. It was at 404 Easy Maywood Avenue, in Peoria, Illinois. One day the neighbors had company, and went out front to talk to them. When they saw our station-wagon, they begged us to trade for their 1953 Chevrolet, two-door sedan. It was baby-blue, and was a very nice car. We traded, and I said, "We are going to drive this till the wheels fall off." The family wanted to see the family in West Virginia before moving because Leo was beginning to get real sick, and when we took him to the doctors, they said he needed major kidney-bladder surgery. One day the family picked me up right after work, and I still had my bowling shirt on. It was black with M & H Equipment of the back of the shirt, in yellow letters. As we were coming into Indianapolis, Indiana, a biker stepped in front of the car. Frances was driving, and came real close to hitting him. We rolled the window down, and he said he just needed a ride about twelve miles to the truck stop to see about getting his motorcycle. He wore black, and said he was a member of the group called, "Hells Angels". I was sitting in the middle, and he was to my right near the passenger door. He looked over to the back of my shirt and the H, and E from my bowling shirt. He said, "What unit of the "Hells Angels" are you with?" I said, The California, "Hell Angels" (Wildcat Unit), the toughest unit around. He was much calmer and better behaved. We talked about going back into the military, so I checked it out and the Army would reduce my grade to E-3, and no choice of assignment. I inquired about joining the Air Force;

and I was offered to retain my E-4 grade, same job, personnel, and choice of base. I was told there was an opening at Holloman Air Force Base, New Mexico. It was near one of the best U.S. Army Hospital at Fort Bliss (El Paso), Texas. I went to Des Moines, Iowa and was tested, and passed all my tests, and enlisted on December 7, 1966. I was working now at Caterpillar Tractor Company, at their print department in Moline, Illinois. I still remember my supervisor, Mr. Lee Wilder, who recommended that I take a four-year leave of absence when joining the U.S. Air Force. We placed the home up for sale, and one day I got a call from the mortgage company about missing three payments in a row. I disputed this, I hired a lawyer, through the base lawyer's and discovered the pharmacist who sold us the home changed the account number to show he still owned the home. I was told we could sue and get the house free and clear. I told the lawyer, we just wanted credit for our payments plus any attorney fees. I got a call one day from Illinois, and the lawyer received the credit for our account. When I asked, "What do we owe?", he said, "Your bill is paid in full because you are serving our country" and "someone in our office is looking into buying your home." America is the only country I know where people will help you like this.

CHAPTER 6

ENLISTMENT IN THE U.S. AIR FORCE

Due to Leo's need for surgery, and job security, I decided to join the U.S. Air Force. The army would reduce my grade to E-3, with no choice of base, and no choice of career field. I went to take tests at Des Moines, Iowa for entrance into the U.S. Air Force. I passed and enlisted on December 7, 1966 for a period of four years. I was assigned to be a Personnel Specialist, and duty at Holloman Air Force Base, New Mexico. The base advised us to admit Leo to the U.S. Army Medical Center at Fort Bliss in El Paso, Texas.

The car that I said I would drive until the wheels fell off. One day I was getting in the 1953 Chevrolet that we had traded, and I was on my way home from work. A Master Sergeant said, "Sergeant, you can't drive that car like that, the left front wheel just fell off." I called a downtown car dealer, and got a super good deal. I traded and received $150.00 for the old car, and paid $400.00 cash for a 1955 Chevrolet, two-door sedan, with automatic transmission. It was blue with a white top. We lived on-base after waiting about six months on the waiting list. I read where the base offered free lumber for base-housing for occupants to build fencing in the rear of our four-unit housing. I arranged for each occupant to help one another until everyone in our complex had a fence with a gate that locked. It was an experience I was very pleased with the results and the cooperation. It is important to help others, and our area was much safer. We were assigned there until November, 1968, and then we were transferred to Sandia Base in Albuquerque, New Mexico. On April 28, 1969, a son was born, Steven Lee Foley at Sandia Base Hospital, Albuquerque, New Mexico. We lived on base and had a very nice three bedroom home with a carport, and brick-fenced back yard. A promotion to Staff Sergeant (E-5) at Holloman Air Force Base was earned in early 1968. I was promoted at Sandia Base in January 1972 to Technical Sergeant (E-6).

Leo got in at U.S. Army Hospital at Fort Bliss, Texas in El Paso. He had his surgery, with Dr. Finder performing the surgery. Many thanks, to Dr. Finder and the entire crew, at the hospital. Leo has grown to be a strong man. I lost track of him after his mother, two brothers, and he and his sister put me in hospice unit after I had a heart attack and caratoid blockage in Birmingham, Alabama in July 1983. I went into a coma on a Friday evening about 6 p.m., and was in a coma about ten to twelve hours. I left the ward, and made it home by the Grace of God. I had a career change, and changed from Personnel to Disbursement Accounting. This was my chance to go to the Accounting School the Army promised me. It was for thirteen weeks, and was held at Sheppard Air Force Base, Texas at Wichita Falls, Texas. I went to Lamar Baptist Church in downtown Wichita Falls, Texas. I was very blessed because I was invited to have Sunday dinner with Christian families in that area, I enjoyed the classes. It wasn't long after I finished school that the Disbursing Accounting merged with the Accounting career. I was special trained in Materiel Accounting which processed all payments and the fiscal accounting records. One of my favorite bases besides Alaska was Minot Air Force Base, North Dakota was my mother's home-state,. It was in Minot, North Dakota, that our son, Phillip Gregory Foley was born on July 31, 1972, We spent seven months there, and travelled to Canada, and the Peace Gardens. I was an active Boy Scout Leader, and Leo was a Boy Scout for about two years. I took the family to Regina, Canada, where we went to the Royal Mounted Police Academy. One day, I called to check on, my sister Mary Lou, and found that she was hospitalized at Saint Elizabeth Hospital in Appleton, Wisconsin. North Dakota was a good state to live, work, and raise children. Mary Lou had a slight heath problem, but we got her in the hospital, and she was much better in about four or five months. She and her son, Billy Johnson, who was almost five years old now, lived with us in our three-story, four bedroom base home. We had a full basement, which we used as a recreation room.

CHAPTER 7

FAMILY LIFE OF GEORGE LEE FOLEY WHILE RAISING CHILDREN

My family life while raising children began on December 5, 1964, when Frances Christian and I were married. She had two children Sandra Bethel Christian and Leo Edward Christian. Sandra was born September 30, 1961 and Leo Edward Christian was born on July 23, 1963. They were born in Albuquerque, New Mexico to Frances Marie and Winfred Christian. Their father passed away suddenly after a brief illness at the age of forty-seven, and had worked as a surveyor. We were a very active family, going to drive-in movies, playing in the park, and playing in the backyard. Our first home was at 364 64ᵗʰ Street N.W. in the northwest section of Albuquerque, New Mexico.

I was transferred from the U.S. Armed Forces Recruiting Station in Albuquerque, New Mexico, and I missed the children. I left in June and they arrived in Okinawa on Thanksgiving Day 1965. I was assigned a two bedroom small house overlooking the Pacific Ocean. The children loved helping decorate, which we did in Japanese-style lamps, candles, pictures, and our furniture was furnished by the base. We had shutters on all the bedroom windows to give us added protection. We soon moved about twelve miles south to Naha Air Force Base Housing. It was a large four bedroom house with a large dining and living room combination, and had a large panel of glass with double-doors, and a screened porch. We had to be very careful because at night, two or three German-Shepherd guard dogs patrolled the entire perimeter of the base. One disadvantage was a Japanese Distillery Company that made wine was across the fence from our house. For added protection; we had an enclosed brick garbage area, about eight feet by eight feet because a monsoon (severe rainstorm) could cause the cans to injure someone. An added safety factor was space in front for two cars. It had lighting at night for protection of our home and car(s). There were parks for the children, movies, skating rink, and bowling lanes. We stayed until July 9, 1966, when my enlistment was over. We bought a 1955 Ford. Four-door sedan, blue and white, when I first arrived, and it only cost $250.00, but we had to leave it there because of the rust, and the excessive cost of bringing it back. We were close to shopping, and we went to the movies with the children, usually every Friday night, Saturdays, or Sunday afternoons. We cost of living was very reasonable. One day I had new spark plugs put in the car, and when I asked for the bill, the mechanic said, "$1.68" I told him I wanted all eight spark plugs, and he said he put in eight new ones. Our $500.00 a month plus paid housing and food and clothing allowance gave us money to enjoy our time and have activities with the children. When our time was up, we departed, July 9, 1966, and arrived at Oakland Army Terminal in Oakland, California for separation from the U.S. Army. I had a very good five years in the service to our country.

As a father to the children, I have always found time to play after work and on weekends. In North Dakota, Sandra and I went to Father and Daughter Spaghetti Dinner, where the daughters would prepare the Spaghetti and the fathers would bring the dessert. In Illinois, our favorite was snow-sledding. In San Antonio, Texas, our favorite was Putt-Putt Golf, and in Fort Walton Beach, Florida it was fishing, swimming, and cook-outs in the backyard. In Alaska, I built a Cross-Country Ski-Slope in our yard. I would have steps for them to climb, and come down on one side of the house, across the front yard and driveway, down the slope into a cleared vacant lot, and back to the steps. When we moved on Elmendorf Air Force

Base, there in Anchorage, Alaska, it was still winter, so we had a double-back yard, since two four-unit apartments were back-to-back. One day I asked the kids ours, and the neighbor kids to get me about ten boards. One night when no one was looking, I made an eight foot by twelve foot rectangular pattern with the boards. On a freezing night, I turned the outside water to fill up the boards with water. In about two days it was frozen. I did the same until we had a large ice skating rink in the backyard. Another on our favorites was, Sandra and I would go a service station that would let us use the water; and she and I would wash the car, since, we couldn't wash it at the house. In Alaska, one Saturday afternoon we went for a drive and off the highway to the left about fifty feet, there was a large glacier. We enjoyed walking on the ice; but as I stepped on one part, it broke loose and I started to float out, with water between the two patches of ice. It was kind of scary. I had to jump about two feet to get off the part that was floating out. Another exciting time in Alaska was when we went to the Ice-Melting Festival, north of

Anchorage. If you could guess when the ice would melt and break the board that was under it, you would win a cash prize. My favorite was the Dog Sled Races, as they came through town. It was called the *"Iteterrod Dog Sled Race"*, and it was really fun for the whole family. This was usually in late January or early February of each year. One other thing that was interesting to see was the "Alaskan Pipeline" that was built in some parts above ground. In Texas, we were active in Boy Scouts, and for Sandra we were active in the Girl Cheerleader Squad. The highlight of our Alaskan tour of duty was the "Aroreya Borrellis" or "Northern Lights"

CHAPTER 8

PHYSICAL AFFLICTIONS OF
GEORGE LEE FOLEY WHILE SERVING
IN THE U.S. AIR FORCE

It was a quiet morning on the path to my place of duty, the Accounting and Finance Office, which was the second hangar from the entrance to the flight-line at Osan Air Base, Korea. I looked to the right and saw three aircraft that were departing the hangar across from my office. There was back-fire from each aircraft; but the one on the left, knocked me to the pavement. It was about February 15, 1973. I should have read the bulletin board in the dormitory. I was told the bulletin board notice was posted for four days. I made eye contact with the mechanic, but when I got to my feet, I thought I was alright. I wandered aimlessly, after checking my hangar, which was my Accounting office, but it was vacated. It was being returned for use as a hangar for assigned aircraft. I suffered substantial memory loss. When I walked the base, I manage to find my dormitory. When I arrived, I was in a state of shock, so I had difficulty relating what had happened. I couldn't speak a word about what had occurred. A Staff Sergeant in my dormitory saw my need for medical care, so we both walked to the medical clinic, about one block away. The medical doctor treating me said I was Lethargic, and near a Diabetic coma. I was listless and was just like a "baby the doctor said" It took about three or four hours to respond. I was released to "Quarters", which means restricted to the dormitory, until released by the medical personnel. The next morning, I went back to the clinic, and the doctor wrote a "consult" to Tachikawa Air Base, Hospital, just outside of Tokyo, Japan. Dr. Wilbur S. Avant, M.D. was my attending physician, while in the hospital. He was the Chief of Neurology, and ran several tests. He found a "seizure disorder" that presented as "Vertigo", and said, I have been an epileptic since birth. It was a rare disorder, Focal Point Memory Loss, and affected my right-side of my head, and "eye fixation", lasting about thirty to forty minutes each episode. I was in the hospital from about March 1 to March 17, 1973. I was given a "four hour pass", and I remember I went to downtown Tokyo, bought a new red and blue silk Japanese necktie, and had a McDonald's hamburger, at a sidewalk restaurant. It was the day the yen went from 360 yen to the dollar to 180 yen to the dollar. Everything doubled in price. I returned to the hospital and was released about three day later. I was told I had this seizure disorder since birth. The doctor said it was a "birth defect". I was released March 17, 1973 to Osan Air Base with assignment to "light duty", for about thirty days, and after completing over fifty percent of my duty, I was assigned to Wilford-Hall Medical Center, the U.S. Air Force largest hospital.

After a few days from being released from Wilford-Hall Medical Center, I saw Dr, Avant in the hallway, and he said he would continue to be my doctor. I was assigned to the Accounting and Finance Officer in the Disbursing Section of Military Pay. I took ten days leave to pickup my family in Peoria, Illinois. I worked in Travel Section, and Military Pay, and Materiel Section.

One Saturday morning, I was shopping at a local home improvement store, and I heard a small voice, saying, "Papason, Papason", which mean Daddy in the oriental languages. It was a small three year old girl that I visited at their orphanage while stationed in Korea. What a surprise! So I wouldn't disturb her, I threw her a kiss, waved, and said, "See you, later" About two weeks later, I saw the Sergeant that adopted her from the orphanage. I was sure happy for the whole family. You can't help but fall in love with those kids. I will always cherish those memories.

CHAPTER 9

STRUGGLES AND OBSTACLES AFTER RETIREMENT FROM THE U.S. AIR FORCE

I retired on December 1, 1981, and went to work for four different local companies: The Okaloosa County School Board, as a janitor for four hour a day, three days a week at Choctaw High School, Fort Walton Beach, Florida. United Parcel Service (UPS), as a janitor with duties operating the cleaning machine and cleaning the bays for three hours, three evenings a week. A private janitorial service at Bell Telephone Company for three hours a day, three day a week, I worked with the Disabled American Veterans (DAV) on-call. I was admitted to Fort Walton General Hospital with a Heart Attack under the care of Dr. Raphael Gomez, M.D. He was very helpful in bringing my health to a stable condition. One thing that was wrong was I had developed Coronary Artery Disease (CAD), and Carotoid Artery Disease. I was sent to Veterans Hospital in Birmingham, Alabama and my first wife, Frances Foley admitted me to the Hospice Unit. I was told they were going to take all my illnesses from me. I was told I was going home on Saturday, and they told me this on Thursday. I found out that James, two beds down was my third cousin. When I asked him for a contact number, I was taken to the Men's Room. As I came out, they rolled a bed with a white sheet, I did not have enough thinking ability to know it was James, but when I got back, there was an empty space where his bed was. I talked with Dewey across from me, and we talked about Heaven, and I looked to the right across from me, and there was my friend

Pastor John Hagee. I met Dr. Hagee in April 1973, when I returned from Korea. I was there right after he had a heart attack at Wilford-Hall Medical Center in San Antonio, Texas. When I asked him if he remembered me he said that he was just there to make sure I was saved, and knew the Lord Jesus Christ as my Personal Savior. I answered, "Yes, I was saved on the island of Okinawa in the early fall of 1965. When I am at an all-time low, I read I John 1 verse 9, "If we confess our sins, He is faithful and just to forgive us of our sins, and cleanse us from all unrighteousness." This verse is known as the security of the believer.

I was at a church service in Panama City, Florida at Saint Andrews Baptist Church in the summer of 1982 with Dr. Jack Hyles from Hammond, Indiana conducting the service, and he made a clear statement that we have the Holy Spirit within us from the time we are saved. On Thursday Dr. Hagee, slipped out of bed in his robe, and entered the Men's Room, and came out dressed in a gray business suit. On Friday after Frances, my first wife came past my bed and said, "Call me when it's over." I said, "Call me when it's over." I did not have a single clue what she meant. About 6:00 p.m., the room became dark, and I began to burn up, as if I had a fever. The medical technician said, "This is how he gets when he is real sick." Then he said, "106". I was in a coma, I could hear, but not respond and it was dark (totally black) until about ten to twelve hours later. I asked the nurse, "What day is it?" She said, "Saturday", I said morning or night, since we were in the basement without windows. I asked if she would dress me like she did James, she did. I then asked for any medicine that I was supposed to take. She said, "You haven't had medicine for about two weeks." I said, "Please mail my medicine to me at my home.", and I left. Before I left, I saw the nurse filling a "needle with some kind of fluid." I was not too coherent, but I knew I was the only one left on the ward. I left the ward immediately. I sat in the Lobby, and I was invited to church service when people started going into the chapel. I could hardly see a thing. I was asked to take up the offering, and when I was done, the preacher said, "You did very well for a "blind man". When the service was over he asked if he could sign me up for the School for the Blind. I said "No, I am going home Saturday,"

The next thing I knew, I guess about next day, a man went up to the counter, and they asked if they could help him, "He said, Yes, I want to go home." I got in line because I thought he could be my neighbor. I was asked who I was, and they checked my wallet, and paid me some money. I followed the man to the bus station and when they checked my wallet, they sold me a ticket to Fort Walton Beach, Florida. I had a quiet ride, and slept until I reached town. I looked to the right and there was K-Mart. I told the bus driver to let me out, please, and he said he had to take me to the bus station. I said, "It would behoove you to let me out now." I didn't even know what behoove means. I got out and walked two blocks to my home at 123 Hummingbird Avenue in Fort Walton Beach, Florida. When I went in my family was extremely angry. They said that they were moving Wednesday because they turned the house back. I felt this cannot be my real family, and my step-son took a swing at me. He said I robbed them of about $30,000.00. I said check my suitcase it may be in there. I didn't know he meant insurance money. I was asked to leave, but refused. I don't know how long I stayed, but went back to work. When they found out what happened they said, "It is easier to promote you to Assistant Manager than retrain you." One day, Frances said "Leave". I rented a mobile home one block from them and one block from work. On my day off, I drove to Montgomery, Alabama, and got a job as a cashier in there on the north side of Montgomery, Alabama. Frances filed for divorce. I went to counseling in Fort Walton Beach, Florida. I moved in March 1986. My divorce was final on August 17, 1986. I started a new life in Montgomery, Alabama and have been very blessed, and much happier. It is hard to believe that I was done the way I was.

CHAPTER 10

VALUES AND BALANCING FAMILY LIFE WITH BUSINESS LIFE

Since I was a very young person, I saw the need for balancing family life with business life. As I grew up to school age, I made sure that I devoted the time to helping in the care of my younger sister, Mary Louise (Mary Lou) to family and friends. There was time for all of homework, on good days there was time for play in the backyard, then there were chores that we each had. Patricia Ann (Pat) to family and friends, went to St. Francis Xavier Elementary School through the eighth grade, then to public school at Lincoln Junior High School, and then to Albuquerque High School. Mary Lou and I went to St. Francis Xavier Elementary School; except for the fourth grade, when we went to John Marshall Elementary School. Mary Lou and I and Pat learned 2ⁿᵈ Timothy 2 verse 15, "Study to show yourself; approved unto God, a worker who does not need to be ashamed, rightly dividing the word of truth." Mary Lou knew this verse was special to her future because she wanted to graduate from her prior school, Albuquerque High School. It was ten years from the time she was supposed to graduate. She graduated in May 1971. She is a remarkable young-thinking person. She has learned to balance family life with business life. In this case, business life was her goal of completing her High School Diploma. My sister, Mary Lou is to be commended for wanting to return to receive her diploma. She did it while raising a son Billy, who was three years old. She has a health set-back, but she quickly recovered and went to work at Steak-N-Shake in Peoria, Illinois. She worked hard and rented an apartment with her son Billy, and she bought a car. Today she is living in Port Huron, Michigan, is a widow, with two grown sons William Johnson (previously called Billy) and Jason Gibson. Jason Gibson lives in Lansing, Michigan with his wife, and one child.

Chapter 11

Motivating and Inspiring Passages from God's Holy Word, The Holy Bible (NKJV)

The Holy Bible written by over forty authors inspired by God is an excellent source for motivation and inspiration in our personal daily living. The book of Psalms was written by both King David, king of Israel, and his son, Solomon. There are several that are my favorites. One special one to me is Psalm 122 verse 1. "I was glad when they said to me, "Let us go into the house of the Lord" The Hebrew word for glad is laughter or delight. The word delight signifies that which brings pleasure to God. The reason is that we enter into the House of the Lord" to bring Praise and Glory to, an Almighty God. We also enter in to sing, as in the days of King David. The Psalms were almost always sung. To me, this inspires and motivates us to a greater service to God, and when we enter in we uplift fellow-believers. We can never repay God for what He has done for us. We were created to bring praise to God and worship Him. Since God is a Spirit, we worship Him in Spirit and Truth. Another one of my favorite verses is Isaiah 40 verse 31, "But those who wait upon the Lord shall renew their strength, they shall mount up with wings, like Eagles, they shall run and not be weary, they shall walk and not faint." In addition to being one of my favorites, it is one of the favorites of many of our church family at Ridgecrest Baptist Church, Dothan, Alabama. I have read this verse many times, and find it to be glorifying to God, and secondly a highly motivating verse from the bible. The entire bible is written under the inspiration of the Holy Spirit. In the Gospel of John, Chapter 4 verse 24, God shows how we are to worship Him. Psalm 119 is a psalm written on the Meditations on the Excellencies of the Word of God. Psalm 119 verse 105, the psalmist said, "Your word is a lamp to my feet, And a light to my path." The psalmist is referring to "light" as a guide for living, and in verse 130, "The entrance of Your words gives light, it gives understanding to the simple" In my life, I recognize how valuable the Word of God is in my walk with the Lord. In Psalm, 125, the psalmist indicates this psalm is a psalm of trust. In verse 1, "Those who trust in the Lord, are like Mount Zion, Which cannot be moved, but abides forever." This is the kind of trust that my life must reflect, and this psalm truly shows that the Lord is the strength of His People. Another scripture verse that I turn to in a crisis situation is. Jeremiah 29 verse 11, "For I know the thoughts that I think toward you, says the Lord, thoughts of peace and not of evil, to give you a future and a hope. A verse of scripture that has a very special message is, Romans 8 verse 28, "And we know that all things work together for good to those who love God, to those who are called according to His purpose."

CHAPTER 12

STRENGTH AND WEAKNESS RECOGNIZED THROUGHOUT DAILY LIVING AND RESULTS IN MATURITY OR IMMATURITY

My strengths and weakness that are very important to having a successful life are discovered by the Prentice-Hall Self-Assessment Evaluation. This test is used widely by colleges, universities, an in the work-place by employers. My first time taking this assessment was in December 2010, while taking a Management class at the University of Phoenix (on-line) towards a Master of Business Administration (MBA) degree. In this assessment, I was evaluated, and I will show the areas that were the most important; however, to take the test yourself, Prentice-Hall will assign you an access code. The website is: www.Prentice-Hall.com. I will show the results, in part of this test, and show how this evaluation, measures a person's strength or weakness. I will explain what these results mean in relationship to the application, is not so much totally of a mature or immature decision-making process.

The items that are disclosed are:

Question   Evaluation

Type A or B   A

Task-Oriented	People-Oriented
or People Oriented	
Sociable or Loner	Sociable
Work on One Project	One
Until Completion or Many	
How do I work with	Well
Others, or do I prefer to	
Work alone	Work with Others

When a person knows his or her strengths, they can improve on them and add to the quality of their daily living. When a person knows the weakness, they can eliminate that which is a distraction or that which hinders their advancement. This applies to yours or mine personal or business life. When a person knows what is required, it is much easier to concentrate on their growth and can monitor their improvement.

These are just a few of the fifty-one Assessment questions in this Self-Assessment Reference: Robbins, Y, Stephen, P. Publisher: Prentice-Hall Publishing Co, Columbus, Ohio

My Prentice-Hall is not a measurement of right or wrong, but a method to determine how; each part is relative to the other, and will evaluate myself in areas of the work-place to determine what style of leadership I have, and whether I am Type A or B personality, level of trust that I place in another person, and many other valuable traits that a person possess. A person never reaches full maturity, but he or she must strive for maturity to be able to compete in a world where there much distraction, competition, and negative thoughts and conflict. If a person does not do anything to overcome this, he or she will soon become a dysfunctional person, and may never get out of a rut or pattern of a nonproductive lifestyle. The use of this Prentice-Hall Self Evaluation is a means to show patterns or things about themselves, that they may otherwise never know. Use it to you betterment and future growth. An important thing to remember when planning your future; be sure to allow for a plan to reward yourself, even if a small way. Take time to reflect of the things that you have done for your betterment, and try to have a support system because if you share your goals, plans and dreams with others, they will seem even more real, and you will experience a greater reward because you have made a difference in your life, as well as the life of another.

CHAPTER 13

SCRIPTURAL PASSAGES USED DURING TIMES OF CRISIS

One scriptural verse that helped me in my Christian Life in Time of Crisis was Philippians 3 verse 13-16 when the Apostle Paul wrote: "Brethren I do not count myself to have apprehended, but one thing I do, forgetting those things which are behind and reaching forward to those things which are ahead." In Isaiah the prophet says in Isaiah 40 verse 31, "But those who wait upon the Lord Shall renew their strength; They shall mount up with wings like eagles, They shall run and not be weary, They shall walk and not faint."

CHAPTER 14

DANGEROUS PLACES AND EXTRAORDINARY CHALLENGES

Life is full of places that are a great danger, and when we are aware of this danger, the reaction from my personal experience is to look for a way to overcome this. My thought process is to accept an extraordinary challenge to relieve the anxiety, and to be able to think clearly. When I was a student, I had to depend upon a bicycle to get to school. It was only a mile to school, and two or three student from the public school would ride their bicycles along with me. And cause me to pass my home by about a mile or more. My family taught me to fight my own battles, so I decided to stand up for myself. This is a policy that should be carried out from the individual, to the national, and to the international level. My chain on my bicycle usually at one time or another would slip off the sprocket, so I carried my large crescent wrench with me. One day, I saw the three bullies, as they were coming, and it happened to be on a day that I had my large crescent wrench with me When IU stripped to put the chain back on, one of them started a fight with me. I immediately struck each one across the back a few times and they fled quickly. It is not our intent to hurt another, but when you stand up for yourself, you gain a greater awareness and you feeling of self-worth will rapidly increase. From that time on I was never bothered with them. Instead of being bothered, they tried several times to be my friend. It was because I had respect for myself, and I did not show fear. I was raised in the 1940's and 1950's and people were more likely to help you when you were in danger. Danger is all around us in our daily living. I made certain on many occasions that I was not in the path of danger, When, I was growing up there were Safe Havens that were not heavily controlled by Government. The reason is this task was sponsored by business or athletic groups. Youth organization, such as the Young Men's Christian Association (YMCA) or Young Women's Christian Association (YWCA) or Boys Club and Girl Clubs. Boy Scouts of America was founded by a British gentleman named William Baden-Powell, and was founded on solid Christian principles in 1905. In 1776, our country was founded on Christian-Judeo principles. It is not a matter of do I care to abide because the laws are in place, and if someone violates these principles, they must face the consequences. They also alert the law-abiding citizen to watch for the dangers, and rely on upcoming challenges that require extraordinary challenges and precautions, so as not to fall victim to these schemes. Danger is all around us, especially in unknown places. We moved from Chattanooga, Tennessee to Clarksville, Tennessee, and pulled into a drive-in fish restaurant. The parking-lot had about forty to forty-five motorcycles. I have nothing against motorcycles because I rode one for over six years. They were there for an Annual Charity Motorcycle Ride. We proceeded with our plans to move there. We looked in the newspaper and found a mobile home for rent about fifteen miles west of the city of Clarksville, Tennessee. This was idea because I had about twenty of my rabbits that I was raising to sell to pet stores and neighbors. We rented a U-Haul truck and car-carrier from Chattanooga, Tennessee. We loaded the family car onto the car-carrier. It was a very well-kept 1978 Chevrolet, four-door that we bought from JoAnne's sister's husband. We rented the mobile home for $400.00 a month, which was a good price. It had one hundred and fifty feet frontal with a circular drive, and brand-new regular windows. We gave the landlord a check for $250.00, as agreed, to hold until payday, which was only two days away. Their son unloaded the household goods and we gave him a check for $40.00 to hold, as agreed. The landlord was the Sheriff of the small town. We went to supper about five miles from there, and we were pulling up in the circular drive, and man began running towards the car and telling us to stop. We saw he had a club, like a short baseball bat, and calling all sorts of bad names. I was so nervous, I had difficulty opening the door, I was so terrified, I could not turn the key to open the He pounded on the door, and told us to let him in or else. We slipped out the side door, nearest the landlord, who said he was the Sheriff, and talked to the lady of the house. The son was listening and came from of one of the bedrooms and said, that was a mistaken identity, he said, "He thought we were the previous family that owed him money." I did not even believe what we were told. The Sheriff's wife gave us a shotgun with about four shells, so we went back to the mobile home. I called Fort Campbell, Kentucky Legal Office (Base Lawyers) and they said to get out of their quick. It was nothing but a bad landlord-tenant problem for months in a row before, and to stop payment, but tell the people you want to have a safe place, and that breaks any prior agreement We weren't on the highway back to town three minutes, and here comes the Sheriffs son and the man that was after us. They followed us to a Motel, but we hid. This time we called a real estate company, where we leased with an Option-to-Buy from an Army Major and his wife, who was a nurse, we looked across the street, and the Sheriff's son was visiting his employer, who was also an electrician. We stayed, but we went to the Dog Pound and got the meanest large Pit Bull/ Yellow Lab mix. That solved our need for protection. To get even, the son saw we didn't take our rabbits, so the Sheriff's wife said "Bring them over and put the twenty rabbits in the extra large cage. I called the Sheriff's wife and told her, we would pay the son and a small fee for the inconvenience. She said "Don't worry, everything is o.k." I felt very bad about owing the family the money, even though we were told we were in the right. We gave them the twenty rabbits to avoid and further conflict. A very important lesson was learned, to go to the base or Better Business Bureau to check things out, rather than do it on our own.

Dangerous places should be avoided, whenever possible, but sometimes it is almost a must. The job situation was very poor at that time. So I accepted an early morning paper-route, which was supposed to last about two months, until the Newspaper office could hire someone permanently. I should have checked out the reason. Even the manager complained that he would not deliver to that area.

It was a very well to do neighborhood. The homes were two and three story, mostly brick homes, with an almost new car in each driveway. I found out the hard way. One morning, I was delivering in my small Opel two door car, that I got thirty miles to a gallon of gas. Well, as I turned the corner, which was a circular street, I looked and saw a motorcycle that was visible and waiting at the corner. He appeared to be stalking me. I had no money for them to rob me of, so I was puzzled as to what was going on. I had a four-speed transmission on the floor. I turned the corner and the motorcycle driver, was trying to run me off the road. It was about 3:15 a.m. I backed off and let the motorcycle driver go ahead of me, he kept going back and forth to keep me from passing him. I said to myself, OK guy you are asking for trouble. I revved my engine, popped the clutch and hit his rear fender and tire, three or four times and then I was going to hit him on his left side of his motorcycle with a light touch, being careful not to hit too hard, but to let him know, that I was not going to tolerate this, which I did. He was weaving and yelling as loud as he could. I struck his back fender again, and he went into a culvert and turned over about two times, and I was aware that there was enough soft shrubbery to cushion his fall. I honked as I went by, all the time revving my engine. I had my window down on the passenger side, and yelled out "This will teach you to Mess With Me," "Do you want another dose of what I just gave you?" I was Combat Trained and trained to handle emergencies. I would lie if I told you I was not scared. I was terrified. But I was justified in what I did to that Stalker.

I went home. Set my alarm for three hours later, when it was daylight I delivered the remaining seventy-five newspapers.

After delivering the seventy-five news papers, I went to get a good breakfast at a nearby restaurant, and when the Newspaper Office opened, I told them what had happened and turned the Paper Route over to them. I have noticed that sometime people want attention, whether for right or wrong.

When I talked to the Police Department, not that I was making a report, and they said that the Newspaper Manager had been a witness to a burglary to a two-story home, and they were after him.

My life seems to have had more than a fair share of dangerous places, and as a result a need to draw on the challenges necessary to not be a total disaster.

I was still on active duty with the U.S. Air Force, and I was on Leave with pay until my retirement date, I was told the off-shore companies were hiring, and for me to travel to Morgan City, Louisiana to get employment. I put new spark plugs in my Opel Kadette, a small two-door German car. I had just tested it for gas mileage. I ran completely out one day, so I put in exactly one gallon of gasoline. I measured it on the odometer and travelled exactly thirty miles. I filled up the tank and set out on Wednesday with the encouragement of my wife Frances' consent and encouragement. (Frances was my wife at that time). When I came back, Frances played the dirtiest trick on me. She went to Calvary Baptist Church, Fort Walton Beach, Florida and told them I left the family for good, so they took up an offering of around $700.00 to $800.00, and all she said was a big lie. I drove to Morgan City where I was told that the off-shore job was two weeks on and two weeks off and the pay was double that of a regular job. When I got there I went to the personnel office where I was requested to apply. I arrived Thursday about 10:00 a.m., and had my Thanksgiving dinner at a chicken restaurant. I almost got a job as a bookkeeper at a plumbing company, but the management was out of town, and only their assistant was sitting in the office. They showed me the company where you apply. I checked in with just a dollar in my pocket left. I was hired, but soon realized this was not my type of employment. I called home to check on the family, but they seemed very cold and indifferent. I was warned that the place was a highly dangerous place because the night before the man who previously occupied my bunk-bed had been murdered. After checking in, I was given a bag-lunch, and bedding. I turned in about 9:00 p.m. because I was really tired. It was a "glorified half-way house". A man eating his supper next to me began shaking when a train passed just a few feet past the parking lot, and he said he wanted to "jump the train". Morning call came, and I went to the dining room about 7:00 a.m., where they issued me another bag-lunch, only with breakfast sandwiches, juice, milk and a fruit. I ate and went back to make my bed. The crew chief came, and I asked if I could work. It sure was different than the work arrangement that I had in the military. I worked four hours, since it was Saturday (from 8:00 a.m. to 12:00 noon). My pay-slip said 4 hours @ $6.00 an hour. Sunday I knew I had to get out of there. When I began packing before going to the office to check-out a older gray-headed man said, "Don't leave until I come back from the store" He came back with a box filled with groceries, and gave them to me. I said, "Thank you". He said "two men will pay you $30.00 to take them to Homa, so they can work there. I said. "Yes, thank you" When I checked out my Pay Slip was: 4 hours @ $6.00/hr. $24.00 Less 2 days @ $12.00/day-$24.00 due: 0

I drove to Homa, Louisiana and the two men were hired there. I travel carefully through the night. I only stopped at lighted Rest Stop along the way. I was on I-10 eastbound and pulled into a Rest Stop, and I saw an eighteen wheeler Moving Van with his hood open. To me that meant the driver was nearby. The driver came out of the restroom, and I asked if I could help. He said, "The engine threw a "rod", and he had to report it to his Moving-van Line Company. I didn't have a problem with taking him for help. "He didn't hesitate to show he his valid work papers and drivers license,", and we stopped at a "truck stop, but there no mechanic that could help. I bought him a cup of coffee, and told him I could take him to a dealer in Pensacola, Florida, and he said he would have the company arrange to pick up his truck. I gave him a ride to a garage that was going to help him. I was turning off I-10 to get to Highway 90. I was about 6:00 A.M. and I would be home in a few hours. It was good to help someone in need. When I need more gasoline to get home, I pulled in a Gulf Station, I looked for my Gulf Gas Charge Card, but I remember I left it at home in my dresser drawer. The owner told me without an authorization from the company they could not help me. When you help someone it will come back to you and it will come back at a much greater degree. I went around the building at the Gulf Station, and called the Gulf Billing Department, and gave them the number to call the Gas Attendant, my account number, amount of gas needed, after verification that I was who I said I was. The Gulf Company called in about ten to twenty minutes, and I was authorized to charge $10.00 in gas, which would more than get me home. God will help, you if you only ask. I heard a preacher say, "You have not because you ask not." Ask in Jesus Name and He will provide. I provided well for my family, and my direct deposit was still going to Frances bank by Direct Deposit. No sooner than I entered the house, she showed me a roll of about $500.00 she had left. How low can you get? The judge at the hearing said, 'She is in need of serious counseling or either she is "criminally insane" I do not judge, but I can examine the fruit of a person's life, and proceed accordingly.

CHAPTER 15

FOREIGN TRAVEL CUSTOMS AND UNITED STATES TRAVEL SINCE JUNE 30, 1961

My foreign travel experiences have been several since June 30, 1961. This is the date I joined the U.S. Army. After basic training at Fort Hood, Texas, I was assigned to complete Advance Individual Training (AIT). This training involved each phase of a combat-related course of training, and I was assigned to train in the M-48 tanks. I went through Basic Training with the 2nd Armored Division, a very highly decorated division during World War II. The 2nd Armored Division has been retired, as a tribute to those who have served "'Faithfully and True." The 1st Medium Tank Battalion, 66th Armored Unit was my basic training unit. I completed basic training in September and M-48 tank training in November 1961. The positions in M-48 tank training were; ammunition loader, .50 caliber machine gun firing, M-60 tank firing, and the final assignment was driver. The M-48 tank weighs fifty-two tons, and it is equipped with a periscope to see the path the driver is taking. I waived my school, due to my loyalty to my unit. I believe if a person makes a sacrifice, it will come back in time. I was cleaning the two 440 cubic-inch tank engine wells, and I had completed one, and I had one to go. As I was crawling out of the engine well, my pant leg and boot caught on the lid of the compartment, and it closed on me. I yelled for help, and two soldiers, a few feet away heard me and came to my rescue. They saw I was scratched up a bit, so they said that they didn't have time to dispatch a vehicle to take us to Graduation Ceremony at the front entrance to the Motor Pool (Base Garage). Two business days later, the Colonel asked me to come to his office. I knew I must be in trouble. To my surprise the Colonel mentioned that an opening was coming up in a month in Finance and Accounting Office, but I could work in the Supply room until then. I went for the interview for the opening in Finance and Accounting Office, and the position was that of Check-writer. My interview involved typing on a manual typewriter a check for the monthly payroll. The check was for $1,000,000.00 (1 million dollars). My monthly Basic Pay was $78.00 as a Private E-1. I worked about six months in Finance and Accounting Office, and then school trained personnel were brought in; but I was given a job that was just as good. I was a Personnel Specialist. In June 1962, Mr. Perry, our Personnel Officer asked me to select twelve office personnel to go to Germany to turn an American tank unit over to the German Army. I asked if I could be one of the twelve, and the Personnel Officer said, yes. We travelled by airplane to McGuire Air Force Base (Mount Holly), New

Jersey. The airplane seats were facing the rear of the aircraft due to better balance, a difference in the force of the plane.

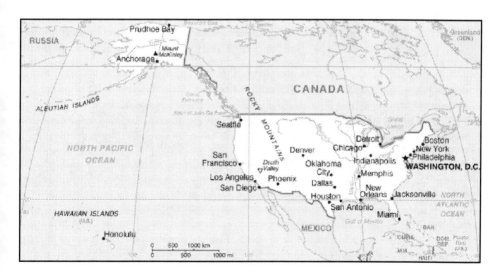

Our stops were Newfoundland, (just to refuel), Dublin, Ireland, Prestwick, Scotland, and Rein-Mein Air Force Base (Frankfurt),

Germany. A military vehicle took us to our new assignment at a small village south of Speyer, Germany. It was about thirty miles south of Heidelberg, Germany. Our duty assignment was from 0700 hours (7:00 a.m.) to 1200 hours (12 Noon). I made the most of my time off. I asked the Supply Sergeant, if I could supply-run. He said, "Yes, as long as I was dressed in my work uniform, and change when I got off the truck, and back to work uniform for the return trip. I went sight-seeing, and I had my "Leica" .35 mm camera, and several rolls of film. I toured castles, museums, wine-cellars, wine-tasting events (I passed on this), but it was in the Mall where I ate a light meal. I went on a train ride one day, and since my mother spoke German to me for my first four years, I could speak some and understand a lot. I spoke with a couple that had a daughter, who was about sixteen years old. I told them my mother was German, and they asked me what her name was. When I told them, they said that was a name very popular in East Germany. That explains why my grandfather changed his last name from "Eickenbrog" to "Eickenbrock". I still have records where my mother's church records show "Eickenbrog".

One day about noon, my friends and I were going into town, so we stopped at the Snack-bar for lunch. I ordered an egg with German bread. I ordered in German. "Egg-mitt-brochen," Danka-shein means "Thank You.", and "Bitte-shein" means "Your Welcome" As I was about to leave one of my friends, said, "Come on, Foley". He then played a song on the Juke-box, It was "Sink the Bismarck" by Johnny Horton. It wasn't too long before then that World War II had ended. We sang their German battleship, "The Bismarck" The two waitresses thought I played that song because my friend ran out right after playing the song.

CHAPTER 16

VALUABLE LESSONS LEARNED ACADEMICALLY AND ON-THE-JOB

Whether you are still in school, just finishing school, about to enter the work-force for the first, or have completed a life-time of faithful service, I hope to give you the insight of the things that will be helpful in the next area of your life. As you quietly think about the lessons that you have learned, and search the needs that you have at this point., and how they can become a reality, I hope I can pass on to you the things that can help you to the next step in your life. After ten years in the military, I realized that I was my own manager, of my career, my choices of education, my family life, recreation, and I could be empowered by my determination to do the things that I thought I could not do because someone said, "You can't do that." When in fact, you can, if you have the determination, I highly recommend that whether you are young or older than others in your circle of friends, you can achieve your goal, and your dreams. You should have at least one mentor in your life at any one time. If you cannot get someone to be a mentor for you, select someone who is a role-model to you and observed what they do to be a success. During the time I was growing up, I had three mentors. A mentor is someone who will guide you in your decisions, until you can develop your plans, and determine your course for your future. It has been said that a person only uses about five percent of their potential. I never thought I would have made a bookkeeper or accountant, or have completed college because

I failed bookkeeping in high school. When I went back to visit after five years, over half of my class had a college degree. It took me over ten years to graduate from the University of Nebraska at Omaha on December 20, 1974 with a Bachelor of General Studies with a major in Business Administration and a minor in Economics. I had a Grade Point Average of 2.88 on a 4.0 scale. I was able to set my mind on doing it. So you can too, whatever your goal or dream may be. One thing I miss the most is the contact with my classmates. I was in a class of one hundred and eight, and can remember almost everyone by name. Someday I will take the time to look up my former classmates, or maybe I will be reacquainted through this book.

EXTRAORDINARY ACHIEVEMENTS,
DESPITE ADVERSITIES

It was not until I was in the military for twelve years that my doctor informed me that I was born with a condition that had made my life extremely difficult. It was revealed to me by Dr. Wilbur S. Avant, M.D., my doctor at Tachikawa Air Base, Japan that I was born with a seizure disorder, which presents as "Vertigo", a rare form of epilepsy, that is known as a "Focal Point Memory Loss", It lasts about thirty to forty-five minutes, and sometimes for just a few minutes. At age nineteen, I slept for over eighteen hours without waking up. To me, this was an unusual and extraordinary achievement to be able to function, as well as I did. I completed high school with a Grade Point Average (GPA) of 2,6 on a 4.0 scale. I also earned ninety semester hours of college, before being placed on seizure medication. In April 1974, I was selected to attend as temporary duty for a period of seven months at the University of Nebraska at Omaha. This was an extreme adversity because I did not have the moral support of my first wife, Frances. She felt that education was not very important. I was dropped off in a motel, and I had to seek my own place for the period of seven months that I was to stay. I rented an upstairs room, not too far from the college for $70.00 a month. I had rented it within two hours after being dropped off. I had my own private bath and could use the kitchen on occasions, such as an electric skillet. I bought me a 26 inch bicycle, brand new red Huffy, and rode it to school, town and it kept me in great shape. I joined a local gym, and I went almost daily. I went to eat about two to four evenings a week at International House of Pancakes (IHOP). My favorite was "Chili-Three-Ways (Spaghetti, Chili and Beans).

I joined a fraternity called, "Pen and Sword" It helped the military who were students. That is where I receive the information regarding the apartment I rented.

CHAPTER 18

CHARACTER GUIDANCE AND ITS' IMPORTANCE TO SUCCESSFUL LIVING

Character Guidance began at a very young age in my life. I was the second of three children in my family, and I was the only son. I have one half-sister, six years older, and one sister, one and one half years younger. My life when I was growing-up was a very secure one because we were a very close family, and as I mentioned in Chapter 2, my two baby-sitters were not human, but were two Doberman-Pincher dogs that took care of me while my family were just a few steps away at their shoe-repair-shop. At six years of age, I weighed only twenty-five to thirty pounds. When Character Guidance is introduced in a child's life at an early age, like myself, their value system is much more helpful in their growth and development. I am speaking on an individual basis, and not on a textbook concept. Somehow this being a part of my life had a bearing on my total outlook on life. I have a very special place in my heart for children, but I have a friendship with pets. This is probably because it requires special training for children. One day, I was watching television; I saw a cartoon where one dog asked another, "Why do you suppose that humans live longer than animals?" "Well" the other dog replied, 'I suppose it takes human longer to learn than it does animals." Character Guidance was a way of life for me in the private school where I went, and in the U.,S, Army, which included it in my Basic Training Course from July 1961 to September 1961 The basic principles for successful living were taught. Our nation was founded on the Judeo-Christian principles, and since you are a part of America this is to be accepted whether anyone accepts or likes it or not, because it is the foundation that our laws, customs, and beliefs are built in our system of lawful authority. Successful living will result because scripture says in The Holy Bible, that if we "sow to the good we will reap to the good, and if we sow to corruption, we will reap corruption.

One thing my mother taught me was be good to your mother and father, and your days will be long upon the earth. Long is determined by God's time-table, rather than man's. We will not depart this earth until our job on earth is complete. Remember when you are going thought a difficulty, you do not know how long, it will be. To me Character Guidance is not a series of lessons, but rather it is a lifestyle.

CHAPTER 19

RESPECT FOR GOD, FAMILY AND COUNTRY

Our nation was founded by a people destined to be free. The most important part of a person's welfare and well-being is establishing a solid foundation of beliefs and priorities. My family taught me at a very young age to have respect for God, family and our country, the United States of America. The order that I was taught is God first, family second and country third.

When a person has for their parents, brothers and sisters, aunts, uncles, and others, they initially have a good respect for themselves. It is very much needed in my life now, next week, next month and next year, because it is something that we constantly need to work at, rather than have it on our minds. Too many friends, loved-ones and acquaintances wander aimlessly, not realizing they have a lack respect for their creator, their parents or their country. As time goes by, it is more difficult for our nation, individually or collectively to be able to make a sacrifice, unless the gain is greater than the sacrifice. I was taught to do one unselfish act toward another, as I saw the need, and you will be surprised at how it will have an effect on not only your life, but on the life of that one person that you have helped. We were greater to give God the Glory that is due Him, and as our Creator, what we do for others, we give back to God. However; we can never repay God for what He has done.

I will always be amazed at the secrecy in the lives of our family, and sometimes friends that the information or knowledge that they change or hide will come out in the future, somehow. My mother was embarrassed by the fact that her mother died giving birth to her. She could not speak about who her mother was. This is no fault of my mother. When I asked about my sister's father, she said he got struck by a train in 1936; but to my surprise, the Genealogy Report showed that he retired from his medical practice and moved to his original homeland, Dublin, Ireland. He lived to be eighty-eight years of age. His father's name was Dan Patrick Kelly, and was a very famous person in Ireland. I was in the U.S. Air Force with two different Sergeants named Kelly, but had no idea that they were related to my half-sister, Patricia Ann., and my half-sister's step-mother was Patricia Ann Kelly, and was a relative to both of the Kellys that are mentioned. One was Alvin Kelly, a Captain that had been passed over for promotion, due to circumstances beyond his control. It was his immediate family becoming "dysfunctional". I could not sit there and do nothing. I gave him an Application to Return to Commission Officer Status. He had nine and one-half years active duty as a Commissioned Officer, and you need ten years to remain on active duty as an Officer. He became a Technical Sergeant (E-6), and I thought that was not a fair outcome. He applied and was accepted to revert to the grade of Captain (03) on active duty and was transferred to the Washington, D.C. area. It was not automatic; his work history was exceptionally outstanding as a Technical Sergeant (E-6). We were co-workers, and this the type of looking out for others that I am talking about. I say this not to belittle a person's past; but to show with a little effort, I was able to help. The difference is that person can retire at the grade of Captain as early as 20 years, rather than wait until he/she has 30 years of military, both active and retire service. The other Kelly was a Sergeant Dan Patrick Kelly. I discovered his grandfather was my half-sister's father according to the Genealogy Report I applied for in 2007. I was the Sergeant in Charge of the section in Military Pay where Sergeant Dan Patrick Kelly worked. It is truly a small world.

By telling this, I have not exposed another to revealing family secrecy because these documents are, in fact, Public Records.

The important thing to remember is to have a good solid priority-system of God, Family, and Country and you will see what a difference it will make in your life.

CHAPTER 20

THE NEED FOR AMERICA TO TURN BACK TO A BIBLICAL LIFESTYLE

My days of growing-up were filled with surroundings of an America that was striving to live for God. From the everyday standard of helping our friends and our neighbors, to everyday common courtesy, America was a nation that still put God first. There is a tremendous need in America today to return to a biblical lifestyle. The beginning of a new era occurred in the 1960's, when the power struggle between the good and evil hit America the hardest. Leaders began to accept and listen to those who wanted prayers out of school. Our nation has forgotten the basic responsibility for educating our children is not the state, but it is the God given responsibility of the parent or parents. The family unit began to be mocked and parental authority was being changed from "Family Orientation" to "Individual Orientation". It was always intended by God for the family to consist of a father and a mother and to replenish the earth by diligently seeking the rules of God and subsequently the plans that God had for us. God made Man the stronger vessel, not to show off his strength, but both man and woman to walk side by side, in their walk; not one in front of the other. This country has made some errors in my estimation, and the one thing that I sincerely feel has caused our country to drift is the elimination of the Draft System. The major downfall that came with elimination is that our younger people no longer cared to leave home to make a life for themselves. It is a joint flaw, not just the parent(s) or the children(s) because remaining at home has its' advantages and disadvantages. Today we have children staying at home until they are in their 30's, 40's or even 50's. Can you imagine s person still living at home getting a membership in a Senior Citizen Organization at their parent's address. I made the mistake of going right off to college after high school, I would have been better equipped if I would have went to a trade school. I was thinking of working hard to better myself. My mother gave me a tool chest for my birthday one year, and when I went to put my tool in it she said, "You can put your tools in that later, but for now, you bring in almost all of your pay from your paper route in coins; about $569.00 in a six-week period of time. I definitely had the discipline for earning my own spending money. I delivered 500 newspapers every morning beginning at 5:00 a.m., and 250 newspapers after school, and on weekends beginning at age twelve, I washed dishes at Henry's Drive In Restaurant on Saturdays and Sundays, and Holidays/. I could not even reach the sink, and I earned $2.00 a day and two meals a day. I was paid every two weeks, and I helped the family. I also sold popcorn, peanuts and cokes and cracker jacks at the Albuquerque City Zoo. I would make about $40.00 a weekend. I loved to ride my bicycle across town, and I would always stop to buy my sister Mary Lou and I a bag or two of tacos and enchiladas. Sometimes I would get a bag of Sopapillas (pronounced So pa pes yas) with honey they were delicious.

CHAPTER 21

KNOWING GOD'S PLAN FOR YOUR LIFE ACCORDING TO THE HOLY BIBLE, PSALM 139 (KJV)

Psalm 139 is God's Perfect Knowledge of Man. This psalm was written by King David of Israel. It is a wisdom psalm of descriptive praise. It was not uncommon in the book of Psalms for the psalmist to mix wisdom and praise. Psalm 139 verses 1-6. "O Lord, You have searched me and known me. You know my sitting down and rising up. You understand my thoughts afar off. You comprehend my path and my lying down. And are hedged me behind and before, And laid your hand upon me; Such knowledge is too wonderful for me; It is high, and I cannot attain it." Verses 1-6, is a description of God's intimate knowledge of His servant, a celebration of God's presence with David . . . a celebration of God's creation of David from the moment of conception, declaration that God's thoughts towards David are innumerable, a prayer for the punishment of God's enemies, a prayer that God might search and lead David

These verses express that God is active to search and test His servant. God know our motives, desires and words before they are expressed. If you make these six verses of Psalm 139 a real part of your life, these verses you will know that these occurrences within our daily lives are allowed by God to strengthen us. Remember that the tests that God brings our way will prepare us to be able to handle better, whatever it is in our lives. It is important to know that while you are going through whatever it is, God is in control. I have called on God many times during my life, and especially in times of crisis; I knew that I was not alone. I knew that a God that loves me loves you too. You will become victorious over the difficulties, and hardships and God will be helpful, not judgmental and not condemning. God promises to put a hedge around you in the presence of your enemies. How can you have a better promise than that? God is a loving and caring God, so if you are going through a test, you must realize that it is only temporary. In the Old Testament, the Book of Numbers, the Holy Spirit gives you a comfort. Tests are usually in groups of forty days. A test is different than a temptation. God never tempts you or I; a temptation comes from the devil. In verse six, King David expresses, "It is high, I cannot attain it" shows that he recognizes the Supreme Power of an Almighty God, King David is saying that he cannot attain it in his own power, but only by the power of God. If you embrace these thoughts, you too will draw closer to God.

CHAPTER 22

DELIVERANCE FROM EVIL MEN ACCORDING TO THE HOLY BIBLE, PSALM 140 (KJV)

Psalm 140 was written by King David to the Chief Musician. All of scripture is inspired by the Holy Spirit. This psalm is to seek God for deliverance from evil men. Those who lurk and seek out to destroy us and hinder us by their violent wickedness, want us to stumble and our misfortune become their gain.

"Deliver me, O Lord from evil men; Preserve me from violent men, Who plan evil things in their hearts. They continually gather together for war. They sharpen their tongues like a serpent; The poison of asps is under their lips, Selah (which means Think about that) Keep me O Lord from the hands of the wicked. Preserve me from violent men, Who have purposed to make my steps stumble, The proud have hidden snare for me, and cords; They have spread a net by the wayside; They have set traps for me. Selah, I said to the Lord "You are my God; Hear the voice of my supplications; O Lord, the strength of my salvation. You have covered my head in the day of battle. Do not grant O Lord, the desires off the wicked; Do not further his wicked scheme, Lest they be exhalted" Selah.

King David of Israel calls on God in his darkest hour; when the enemy seems to be succeeding, but God in His Infinite Mercy,

66

comes to his defense, and He will do that for you, if you accept the Lord, as David acknowledges God as the strength of his salvation in verse 7. I have called on God numerous times to deliver me, and give God the Glory for being the strength of my salvation." May God Richly Bless You and you families and keep you from evil men.

CHAPTER 23

NEWS, SPORTS AND WEATHER

Life is really full of exciting things; my experience over the years has shown that the subject of this chapter is a very important one to living a balanced and healthy life. News is very important in keeping up with recent things in our daily living. A person will have a happier life if these three are an active part of their life Too many people today, do not have a hobby; so to keep life interesting I have about four or five at any one time. I will change how long I spend on one, and I always try to not cause any neglect in my personal interaction with people. I enjoy doing Genealogy Studies (Study of Family History), Computer Games because they keep your mind fresh, alert, and sharp, I enjoy repairing old furniture, especially old rocking chairs, I enjoy sports of all kinds; Baseball, Basketball. Football, and especially Hockey because of the speed at which it is played, I enjoy collecting old knives, clocks, and Indian ceramics, and old artifacts. I enjoy making 8 x 10 framed poetry or old writings about historical events, hunting, reading, and lately authoring books, of which this is my first. I hope to do educational textbooks in Business and History, true story hunting, adventures that I encountered in Alaska, New Mexico and North Dakota. I find when you have an active interest in these three News, Sports and Weather it build a common bond in people around you, and you learn about people, their goals, accomplishments, and even creates a pride in belonging. Have you noticed, not one sports card will tell any bad news about a player, and it accentuates the positive, and eliminates the negative.

When you watch Sports News, if any bad news at all such as an injury, it is usually followed up by how soon a person/or player can make a positive comeback. I heard a speaker once say at our church, "Failure is nothing more than succeeding at the wrong thing. A person who makes his profession as an announcer of News, Sports or Weather can verify that a person can do thirty things that are newsworthy, but make one mistake they will be remembered by that one mistake. To me this can be called "Shooting your own wounded"

I once heard of a coach on the west coast, and he was an excellent coach, leader, motivator, and excelled in bringing out the best in all his athletes. He had led his team to a six straight winning season, and was about to renew his ten year contract as coach of a major team. He just turned seventy years of age, and asked if he would sign for another ten years, he without hesitation said, 'Yes" and he signed. The ten years went by and the team was still undefeated. They said "Coach, Are you ready to sign for another ten year contract?" He would soon be eighty years of age. He said, "I have thought hard and long and prayed about it; but I think I will turn it over to a younger man." I was told that was the story of the famous coach, Coach Skaggs.

CHAPTER 24

MY MISSIONARY JOURNEY, A LIFELONG COMMITMENT

My Missionary Journey-

Foreign-Missionary Specialist (E-4) George L. Foley, RA1859 4588, U.S. Army, Fort Buckner, Okinawa

Okinawa from July 1965-July 1966

Tokyo, Japan from March 1-17 1973

Korea from October 1972-April 1973

I was led by a U.S. Army Chaplain at the Fort Buckner, Okinawa Chapel in the early fall of 1965, to the Lord Jesus Christ after confessing my sins, asking Jesus to come into my life and by His shed blood on Calvary, my name was written in the Lamb's Book of Life. I went Soul-winning in October 1965, and led a Japanese student to the Lord Jesus Christ in the Spanish language, which we both spoke fluently.

October 1995 Listened to Dallas Christian

Radio program with Marlin Maddox, who interviewed a former Japanese student of Religion at Naha, Okinawa, and was led to a saving knowledge of the Lord Jesus Christ in October 1965 by an American soldier in a language, both the student and soldier understood, together. Maddox stated former student became Prime Minister of Okinawa, returned island to Japanese control, rid of island of Communism and promoted the Christian Faith throughout the small island of Okinawa, Japan.

CHAPTER 25

RECREATIONAL PLACES REVISITED AND THEIR IMPORTANCE IN MY LEARNING, MY CREATIVITY AND ITS' BENEFIT TO SELF AND OTHERS

In your circle of friends, like mine, I find it hard for people, myself included to take time to enjoy the things they have earned. My life has not been a materialistic one, nor would you say a religious one. The reason that it is not either one is that if I spent my life trying to become a wealthy person, it would be apparent in my goals, and motives for accomplishing things. I could not be a manager, or a business owner that is both task-oriented and people-oriented. Religion is not the labeling of a person that thinks about church, but to me, a person, instead of religious should be spiritual or spiritually-minded. First and foremost, a person should strive to live a balanced life. My doctor told me not too long ago to take a two-week vacation. It is difficult to take the time for relaxation, to devote our valuable time to set it apart from our busy schedule. I asked a friend if they would visit a mutual friend, they said, "I am too busy: They were absolutely right; they are "too busy" We all have the same twenty-four hours day. What they are saying that "It is not important to me."

My travels have done more than just let me see different things that another person had not had the opportunity to see. If a person does not have the proper rest, proper amount of time from his or her job, it will show. God designed our bodies when he created us to have one entire day of rest, and eight hours of sleep for the average person. My life has been such that I have almost always had an interest to travel to new places, and especially revisit places that I have been to in the past. This day and time a person can be obsessed with the economy, the amount of money left-over at the end of each pay period; but I have always been a person that is optimistic, a person that looks for the best in any and all outcomes. My life is getting better, not worse is the right attitude to have. Someone once asked me "Why do I look depressed, and seem unhappy" Sometimes they mistake depression with suppression. Depression is "Nothing to look forward to"

Suppression is being held back from a goal or dream, or something that a person has had his heart and mind set on doing or getting done in a certain period of time. When a person spends time at a recreation related activity they develop their minds, as well as their bodies. Doing this a person may develop a new talent, or use an existing talent before they lose it. If I am not careful and isolate myself, I may lean toward become a "hermit" or develop a personality that is extremely hard to bring back to a "normal balance"

I enjoyed visiting my hometown of Albuquerque, New Mexico. Today there is a park where the old famous Fred Harvey Hotel once was. Old Town was not the same as it was when I was there lat time, a casino on the east part of town is part of the growth that has taken place. One thing that really amazed was the old home at 1604 Arno S.E. When we drove into the neighborhood, I did not see one person on the street, or in any yard, it was quiet.

The high school I attended, St. Mary High School was now part of the Anglican Church Fellowship Hall.

We went south to Roswell, New Mexico, when our niece and nephew, Marissa and David Hrisco were married, and we went to Ruidoso Downs. New Mexico. This is another place that I have revisited. My first time here I was helping the Anderson family build the foundation for my friend, Roberta Anderson's brother, who was stationed at the Air Force Base in Roswell, New Mexico. When it was lunch time I was asked to go to the Chicken Shack about a block away. I had all of my order written down. As I entered the tiny diner, I saw a gentleman, with long silvery hair, and black eyeglasses sitting a table, and he had on an apron so I knew he worked there. The cook came out of the kitchen, and said, Colonel Harlan, if you want me to teach you to fix that chicken before you go back to Kentucky; you need to come to the kitchen. It was Colonel Harlan Sanders, himself. Before he went to the kitchen, he finished his coffee, and said, I will soon be seventy-two, and I do want to learn, so please have patience with me. I am gonna make it. I am gonna make it. I was honored to have met the Colonel. It reminds me of some of my ventures, I am going to be seventy-three years of age this next June. I wish you and your entire family the very best there is in life.

CHAPTER 26

THE FOLEY FAMILY PETS SINCE 2003

Over the past ten years, JoAnne and I have rescued about twenty dogs. We began in 2003, but we were given a beautiful Chow/Golden Retriever Mix in 2002. She had lived at the Sonic Drive In Restaurant in Kaufman, Texas for two years before she was given to us, and we named her Pretty. She is now thirteen years old, and she is a real good pet. Our neighbor to the rear of our home had about twenty head of cattle, and one donkey that was a Nanny to the cattle. One day, I said "John what is your donkey' name. He said, 'I can't tell you, it a secret. "Why is it a secret? I asked. He said, "He understand Spanish and English so be careful what you say to him" One morning, I said, "Hey, Pedro". Well I thought that donkey went crazy, he punched about six cows, and tore up four boxes. I told John what happened and asked if his donkey went crazy. John said, "What did you call him?" Well, I just said "Hey, Pedro" When you said "Pedro, he thought you said "Perro", and that means 'Dog in Spanish and he hates to be called a "Dog". We continued to enjoy our two acres in the country on John Wayne Road.

When we lived there in the country on John Wayne Road, our maintenance man, James built us a six compartment fenced yard, that was off the side of our home, and had a ramp, which was screened, so the pets could run down the ramp to their fenced-yard. It had a six by ten foot shelter to protect them from the rain.

Some people thought we were the Kaufman County Animal Shelter, but that was alright because we loved our pets, and would find a good home for them as fast as they could drop them off. We still had a long-hair beige male Chihuahua, male named Muffin, and a black and white Shed-zu, male named Maverick. Muffin lived to be sixteen and one half. Maverick lived to be sixteen years old. We rescued a one-hundred pound Australian Cattle Dog on Highway 21, who was running down the middle of the highway after someone let him out of their truck. We called the owner, who said we can keep him. We named him "Little Boy", and he lived to be fourteen and one-half years old. He was with us until 2010. The lady next door gave two, six month old Labrador pups, and the male was black and white, so we named him Spot and the female was medium brown, so we named her Sissy. A lady that lived two doors over came up in the driveway with her Bassett Hound, a male, and since we lived on John Wayne Road, we named him Duke. The lady next door told us whose dog it was, so I wanted to be sure she didn't want him. I asked her and she was crying, I heard her husband at the door, saying we can't have him, we couldn't

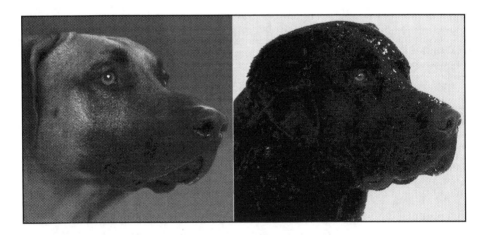

buy the material for keeping the dog in the yard. We gave the two six month old Lab pups to the Highway Department/Roads/ Grounds/Pavement Supervisor, and he sure was happy. He said, He was single and they would be like his new family. We gave Duke to a lady who had just lost her husband, and was a new widow. Friends in Montgomery wanted a small chow/mix and we adopted her from the Animal Clinic. She was only three months old and a truck pulled up at a convenience store and they really wanted her, it was o.k. since the couple that we got her for, changed their mind. Then one day, we were going to the next town, north of Kaufman, Texas, Terrell, Texas to the bank. I looked to the right and said to JoAnne, "Look there is a sheep caught in the bushes in that field. Let's stop and set if free. I looked closer, and it was a gray matted dog about two years old. We said we just can't keep it now, so we took it to the Animal Shelter. They said if no one claimed it in 72 hours, we could have it if we wanted. We picked it from the Dog Pound, and took him to our Animal Clinic. They groomed him gave him his rabies shot and a bath. When we went to pick him up, we said, 'Are you sure that is the dog we brought in?" He was a Brown and White Springer Spaniel about two years old, and looked like a "Champion Show Dog." We named him Dusty. The next visit they said, "I see why they dropped him off in the field because he has heartworms". A lady veterinarian said she would get rid of his heartworms at a very low cost. He got better in about four month. A lady at another Animal Care Center fell in love with and she had a Cocker Spaniel that needed a friend at home to play with. We also rescued a Pit-Bull Lab that we thought was just Labrador, her name was Oatmeal and they were coming just around the corner to pick her up and her "put to sleep", We gave her to a farmer, who need a good guard dog. We have at our home a female Retired Police Dog, Rottweiler/ Labrador mix. Black, female; who lost one eye in the line of duty, catching some illegal drug dealers, and she helped them to justice. She was a "\Drug Detection" dog. We call her Lucky, but out of respect, we call her "Officer Shadow". Lucy is a female German Shepherd/Yellow Labrador mix that was owned by our nephew, and instead of placing her in a good home, he just let her roam free. She had ten puppies who were taken from her early when she had them under a neighbor's porch. Lucy and Lucky are the best of friends, and they are really good guard dogs. I am going to try to have their pictures included in this chapter. When these pets have lived their lives out, we will not replace them. They are just like family. I am going to end this chapter with a Dog Joke. My step-son one day said to me "Why don't you do everything my mom says?", "Easy, I am Half-German, and very stubborn, and what is the other Half of You, he asked?" I replied. "Shepherd" May God Richly Bless each of you is my prayer."

REFERENCES

Robbins, Stephens P., Prentice-Hall, Self-Assessment, Library 3.0

The Holy Bible Isaiah 40 verse 31, Philippians 3 verses 13-16, Psalm 46 verse 1, Psalm 119 verse 105, Psalm 125, Psalm 139 verses 1-6, Psalm 140, verses 1-8, 2nd Timothy 2 verse 15., I John 1 verse 9, and Psalm 122

University of Phoenix College, Phoenix, AZ (On-Line) Transcript issued to George L. Foley MGT 521 Management 3 Semesters Hours, Master of Business Administration (MBA) Candidate (2011)

Westwood College, Denver, CO (On-Line) Transcript issued to George L Foley. 13.5 Credit Hours, Master of Business Administration (MBA) Candidate (2010-2011)

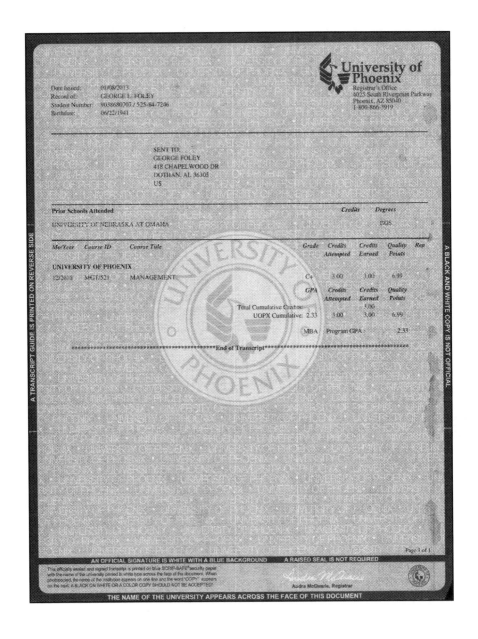

University of Phoenix

Registrar's Office
4025 South Riverpoint Parkway
Phoenix, AZ 85040
1-800-866-3919

Date Issued: 01/08/2013
Record of: GEORGE L. FOLEY
Student Number: 9038680707 / 525-84-7246
Birthdate: 06/22/1941

SENT TO:
GEORGE FOLEY
418 CHAPELWOOD DR
DOTHAN, AL 36305
US

Prior Schools Attended		Credits	Degrees
UNIVERSITY OF NEBRASKA AT OMAHA			BGS

Mo/Year	Course ID	Course Title	Grade	Credits Attempted	Credits Earned	Quality Points	Rep
UNIVERSITY OF PHOENIX							
12/2010	MGT/521	MANAGEMENT	C+	3.00	3.00	6.99	

		GPA	Credits Attempted	Credits Earned	Quality Points
Total Cumulative Credits:			3.00		
UOPX Cumulative:	2.33		3.00	3.00	6.99
	MBA	Program GPA:			2.33

**************************************End of Transcript**************************************

University of Phoenix College, Phoenix, AZ
(On-Line) Transcript issued to George L. Foley

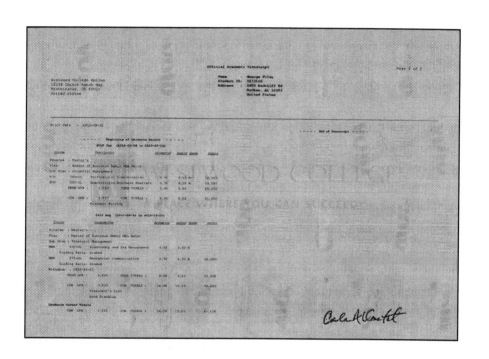

Westwood College, Denver, CO (On-Line)
Transcript issued to George L Foley.